I Used to Love My Business Now I Hate It!

Mike Wolf

authorHOUSE®

AuthorHouse™
1663 Liberty Drive
Bloomington, IN 47403
www.authorhouse.com
Phone: 1 (800) 839-8640

Published by AuthorHouse 04/10/2019

ISBN: 978-1-5462-1562-2 (sc)
ISBN: 978-1-5462-1560-8 (hc)
ISBN: 978-1-5462-1561-5 (e)

Library of Congress Control Number: 2017917036

Print information available on the last page.

This book is printed on acid-free paper.

To Jennifer,
who is the mirror of my soul in everything I do.

To Kristin Kopp, the CEO: Chief Editor of Operations
for everything we touch. And the best business partner
I could ever be blessed with.

To the 72 executives of global companies
who gave generously of their time
to give me the knowledge to write this.

To Ed and Bev Puzia, who had enough faith in me
to put their entire company on the line
as a Kanketa research laboratory.

To all the small businesses owners
throughout the world who had the courage
and commitment to follow through
with the Kanketa principles.

To the brilliant Michael Tincher
You've helped me in ways you'll never know.

To all of you, I am eternally grateful.

Contents

Every business problem that exists, or has ever existed, is the
result of one area of a company out of balance with another.
All solutions can be found by putting the
company into balance with itself.
Solve the problem internally, and the external forces will follow.
Balance the company, and you will solve the problem.

KANKETA ("Journey in Balance") is a proven
prescription for business success.
Kanketa is the science of small business management.

—Mike Wolf

Preface

So, you own a business, do you? Well, then, at least one of these might sound familiar.

"I'm a Startup. Big on ideas. Small on resources."

"I'm just going. Not growing."

"I'm fighting to rescue my failing business."

"If only I could retire with enough money . . ."

What if, right now, at this very moment, your business struggles could be over? What if you could eliminate all the stress, frustration, and guesswork of persistent money problems, tax issues, undeserving lowball competitors gnawing at your heels, unpredictable, unforeseen economic swings, and the like? What if you had a crystal ball that actually worked and could forecast your outcome with incredible accuracy?

"No, thanks. I'm good for now. Our business has never been better. We just can't fill orders fast enough. We're growing by leaps and bounds."

Really? True, or truth? Perception or reality? What measurements are you taking that make you so certain?

In my story, you might see your business differently. If you allow yourself to recognize that there are proven processes and tools that you might not know of that can help you to enjoy the much deserved rewards that your business has to offer . . .

It might be time to consider a whole new way to own your business.

It's all about choice. No judgements. Just decisions, and consequences.

I USED TO LOVE MY BUSINESS

I used to be an ardent fan of my business. I simply couldn't wait to get to work. It was hard to believe that I was financially rewarded for doing what I loved. I had a handful of delighted customers and I served them well. I had three employees and we were more than a business. We enjoyed each other and operated like a family.

. . . NOW, I HATE IT!

Then, the business grew. The money (and loss of money) grew. The product line grew. The smallest of employee issues were now exploding into the biggest of problems. My paycheck was being held under tight security in the petty cash drawer. Between five minutes a week with my family and going AWOL for a gasp of air (I put my health on hold), I would constantly wonder if the light at the end of the tunnel was a train. The business wasn't predictable. Constant changes always hurled me back to the starting line, robbing me of my personal time. The only thing that was predictable was the stress, the mystery, and the guesswork.

The business I used to love felt like a gooey vat of peanut butter that I could never climb out of.

I Felt Like I Was In A Boxing Match

My customers began to bounce me around like a rubber ball, doing whatever they wanted to do at will, paying whatever they felt like paying whenever they felt like paying it. We were lower than the lowest on the totem pole.

Our suppliers weren't much better. They took their own sweet time to get us our critical supplies. Promised due dates were ignored. Calls weren't returned. Invoices were messy. The only guarantees we could absolutely count on with any degree of reliability were delivery errors. It only took one little complaint to turn what should have been a pleasant supplier experience into a combat zone with an archenemy. On occasion, we were held for ransom when we were only a few days late with a payment. Customer service became "Customer nervous."

Employees bickered. The office morphed into a political battleground. There always seemed to be the fight of the day in progress over the smallest things. Bills were piling up faster than the profit came in to pay for them. Debts mounted. Payroll was a struggle, but I didn't dare let anyone know out of fear they'd leave me. Our banker stopped sending us baseball tickets. Instead, he paid routine visits to ask if we would be making our loan payment on time.

Around my then wife, Sally's, career as a third-grade teacher, she had all she could do to keep the boys fed, clothed, and intact. She could only listen to my problems and complaints and offer empathetic support.

My fun little company turned into a boxing match. I felt like it was me against the world. It was ugly. It was debilitating. And I didn't know how to fix it.

I knew I had to take immediate action. Perhaps a college refresher course would do the trick. The brochure promised to give me the exact training I was missing. I called the college to check out the available evening classes. The college curriculum coordinator tried to be helpful, but we both knew it wasn't going to work.

"Let's see, so what we have is two one-hour classes in finance over eight weeks, and you might want to think about the Employee Relations class on Monday and Thursday evenings from seven to nine."

My business was sure to collapse long before the end of the third business theory lecture by some professor who never owned a business.

I began to realize that I was hopelessly chained to my business. Even if I did find the right classes and the right instructors with the right schedules, I knew there was a darn good chance I wouldn't have the time, interest, or ambition to follow through. I was landlocked.

Business Is Like Boxing

To many of its avid fans, boxing is a sweet science. They are out to convince you that boxing is the most challenging of all sports. Boxing demands speed, agility, finesse, power, endurance, and ultimate mental toughness. Boxing pushes you like no other sport, pitting the finest and highest-level athletes against each other. Perhaps these might be the benefits through the lens of the boxing crowd, but to some of us, boxing is a raw and brutal sport.

I'm not a fighter by nature. Rocky Balboa on TV with a bowl of popcorn was the only boxing I watched growing up. Mom wouldn't let us watch Saturday night fights. She thought they were disgusting, violent, and downright repulsive. And yet, all I can think is that boxing is the handiest metaphor to describe my early business experiences.

Business Is A Fight

Later, when I went into my own business, I'd routinely be seen with a black eye and a bloody lip, drained of energy after fighting my way through the tough problems of the day.

Business has its unforgiving rules, its opponents, its risks and returns. There are winners, losers, and spectators. And, yes, the winners get trophies, often at a questionable expense. Business is a fight that goes on every minute of every day in companies across the globe. Families are fighting for ownership. Managers are fighting over budgets. Customers are fighting for deals. Owners are fighting for their profit. Vendors are fighting for the owner's attention. Employees are fighting with each other. Companies are fighting for market share. Customer Service is fighting with customers. Everyone is fighting for position. Collectors are fighting with debtors. It's all a big fight. It's miserably exhausting, usually damaging, and downright debilitating.

The Fight For The Life Of My Business

I was tired of fighting. Extremely tired. Tired of being the brash, bullheaded, "rather be right than rich" fighter that I was. Tired of investing in quick snake oil answers from books with alluring titles, only to find that I would skim over pages, thumbing them through for any immediate quick tip of the day that would save me before I tossed the book into the trash. Tired of celebrating an occasional good moment here and there. Undeniably, my business owned me more than I owned the business.

I finally reached in and grabbed at my soul. I was in the fight along with everyone else. I was engaged in the fight between my company, its income, its debts, and its survival. I knew I must either come out on top or abandon everything I believe in and stand for.

Put Up Your Dukes!

If you have a business of any size or type, you have debt. And, if you have debt, your decision to be in the fight has already been made. You're in the ring. You might have only been in the ring for a minute, or perhaps for decades. But you will either win, or lose.

This book is about the fight for the life of your business.

Now, you might simply love to fight, and look at your business as a boxing match. You might enjoy the challenge of putting your gloves on every day to punch through the walls and punch out a profit. If so, then do what you must. My story probably won't interest you. On the other hand, you might be feeling that the business you once loved is chewing you up and effortlessly spitting you out. Slug after slug, a little voice is telling you to keep fighting and taking it on the chin. You constantly hear a worn and dated broken record of motivational speeches that roll around in your head. "Never give up. Your business won't be worth anything if you don't work hard. Your father wouldn't have done it that way," and whatever else pounds through your brain.

If you are among the many owners who are worn down and fed up with the constant weary struggle of owning a business, then read on. You'll be glad you did.

CHAPTER 1

GITMO DEBT IS BACK IN TOWN

I heard the buzz. The word on the street was that Gitmo Debt was back in town and he was coming after me. He had a score to settle and he was looking for a fight. I've heard rumors about this character before, and today he's showing up on my doorstep.

Clearly, Gitmo Debt is no lightweight. Over the years, he's threatened my business, and the businesses of my friends. His world heavyweight title, "Champion of Business Destruction" precedes him. I've managed to squelch him a few times before, but this is the first time I will get a real close look at him. I've read up on his fight record. He's built quite a reputation for bullying folks. Says he single-handedly takes down 380,000 businesses every year without breathing heavy.

The Day The Earth Stood Still

It started out like every other day. I was my usual restless self after a night of sporadic, interrupted sleep. I traded my usual sit-down breakfast time of long ago for my two-minute grab-'n'-go blueberry muffin and black coffee. Today I came in early with my typical agitated stomach about what had to get done. It was payroll week, and the only thing I was looking forward to was the mail, to see which of my customers were kind enough to pay on time.

As I meandered to my office and started to peruse through the day's long work list, my bookkeeper placed a piece of paper onto my desk. "Accounts payable due this week." She managed to slip a pink sticky note on the back. Susan knew I wouldn't like what it said and she wanted enough time to evacuate my office. The sticky note read: GITMO DEBT IS HERE. I HAVE LOTS OF ERRANDS TO RUN. SEE YA LATER. Susan bolted briskly out the door.

"Hey, what's this?" I yelped. My eyes became glued to the page. Gitmo Debt had arrived at our office and he wanted to get up close and personal with me. As I began to pull myself together, there he was, outside my window, staring right at me.

Gitmo Debt

OMG. YOW!!! Double Yow. It's really . . .

At first glance, I couldn't believe my eyes. He was big. No . . . he was unbelievably huge! He was gnarly. And he was for real. What an ugly sight! This was the first time I actually laid eyes on him. I had no idea how big and beastly he really was.

"Is this the Gitmo Debt I've been fighting with for all these years?" I gasped.

Needless to say, I didn't invite him in. As I poured over the payables, I could almost smell his foul breath in the room without even opening the door.

I paraded frantically through my bills. Most were past due. I was making promises I couldn't keep, just to stave off my suppliers for another week. I was living on the hope that the suppliers would sell me just enough to keep our business open long enough for the next miracle to happen. It was a grim situation. My eyes toggled between the payables and Gitmo's ugly grin. He was really enjoying every moment watching me squirm. I was miserable through and through, and he knew it.

From time to time I've lost small skirmishes to him in the past. And no, I didn't always escape unscathed. But that was early in the game, when I was first putting my business on the map. Back then, the small debts in my little company were minuscule, and much more easily managed. Gitmo always seemed to be just a nuisance; but today, he's a big threat. My heart started pounding. Perspiration drenched every inch of my shirt.

Whatever became of that business I used to love? When did the passion disappear? A few months ago I was enamored with the idea of moving my little-ol'-me business out of my basement and onto street level. I beamed with pride knowing that my company was finally bigger than me. I found myself greeting actual employees in the morning. My business was bigger. My plans were bigger. My expectations were bigger. The money was bigger. The customers were bigger. The rules were bigger. And, yes, my debts were bigger . . . way bigger. In fact, they were dauntingly insurmountable. I had entered a new, bigger arena. It all caught me completely by surprise. In retrospect, I just didn't realize what I was getting into. It all looked so good on the surface.

It's harder than I thought. Why don't I just close up shop and get a job? No, I could never do that. How many people would I let down? If I threw in the towel, I would be ridden by guilt. Anyway, getting a job would never do it for me. I'd hate myself worse for giving up. I was stuck in a quagmire of confusion. I didn't have enough investment money to be the best, and my pride would never allow me to be less. I was in a tug-o'-war with myself that I wasn't winning.

If the truth were known, I was unprepared as hell. I had my head in the sand for so long, doing what I loved, attending to my own little needs, that I didn't really learn the first thing about how to run a company of more than just me. The day we moved into our offices, everything changed. I was no longer that nice little guy who gave away freebies and volunteered for non-paying community projects just to get his business noticed. At that moment, I became responsible for the lives of other people. All of that swiped me upside the head, big-time.

How on earth would I ever be able to stand up to this Gitmo gargoyle? If I didn't get help soon, he would mop the floor with me. Make no mistake. He was there to take me down, along with all the gory business details that I'd been ignoring for so long.

One thing was absolutely certain. Right then, I knew that I needed the best trainer I could find, with the best techniques I could find, in the best gym I could find, as fast as I could find him. Customer reports were due and they continued to pile up, but my mind kept wandering off the pages. I was frozen in my tracks. I sank into a wave of depression. Anxiety and a feeling of helplessness danced over me. "Paralyzed" was another ripe synonym. I mentally shut down and couldn't work for the rest of the day. This big debt thing was out of my league. I didn't know the first thing about fighting Gitmo Debt at this level.

I made up some lame excuse to my team, closed the office early, and went home. There I sat, staring at the wall of my man cave. My appetite was nowhere to be found. I hit the couch and began flipping through TV channels. Nothing grabbed me.

Then, the voice in my head took over. "Hey, this isn't you. You're always the positive and upbeat one. You've got to snap out of it." Without another minute of hesitation, I powered up my laptop and went online to search for anything to help.

"Let' see . . . Google . . . search . . . trainers . . . hmmmm. Trainers, coaches, business . . ." It took 18 minutes for my frustration level to peak. It was finally at the 11ᵗʰ page of business coaches that I had to stop. It seemed like everyone and their mother was a coach. How would I ever pick through all this rubble? I wrote a couple of want ads and placed them generously onto some popular business web sites.

> Wanted. Reliable, experienced business coach
> who knows what in the hell they're doing.
> Strong background in finance is a must.
> Those not bringing immediate results need not apply.
> Must come with references.

My eyes were getting droopy and I started to see dark spots. It was late. I was exhausted. I must have really needed some shut-eye because I was asleep in less than a minute after my head hit the pillow.

CHAPTER 2

THE RIGHT TRAINER FOR THE RIGHT FIGHT

Then, something happened that I didn't quite expect.

In the words of the Buddha, "When the student is ready, the teacher will appear." A teacher did appear. The teacher taught me a better way to own a business. A respectful, less stressful way. A pull, not a push. A way in which everyone could always win—my customers, my employees, my vendors, my family, and most of all, me. The teacher armed me with a bulletproof prescription for finally fixing my business once and for all. What I learned was more accidental than intentional. I would never have found it by searching. The instruction that came to me was elusive to many small businesses. In fact, it was almost under the exclusive protection of the large corporate community. There was no library or college, no mentor or seminar that I would ever have learned it from. It was pure happenstance that it made its way to my little company.

The Teacher Appeared

It was eight thirty-five the next morning when I first looked at my cell phone. The sun poured through the window and touched every object in the room. I had fallen asleep on the couch with my now wrinkled clothes on. Between my buttons and the creases in my shirt I looked like an accordion. I couldn't get motivated to go into work. I noticed that I'd slept through a call from a number I didn't recognize. "Unknown Caller" was lit up on my caller ID. I was ready to send it sailing into the techno trash when it hit me. In my stupor, I had momentarily overlooked that I had used my cell in my want ads as the number to call. No one I didn't know had my new private cell number. This confirmed that it wasn't a telemarketing call. My curiosity took over and I hit the redial. After four rings, a crackly voice with a slight Asian accent answered. It sounded like he might have been from Japan.

"Hello."

"Hello . . . ? You called my cell number."

"Yes. I saw your ad for a business coach, trainer."

"Who am I speaking to?"

"My name is Kanketa"

The introduction was rather clumsy. At first I found him abrupt and to the point. "Well, tell me, do you have a first name?" I inquired.

"Just Kanketa will be fine. What do you need?"

"So . . ." I replied. "I'm looking for someone to train me for a fight."

"A fight?" he asked. "What kind of a fight?"

I paused. "I am going into the business boxing arena."

"And . . . who are you fighting?" he queried.

I answered with some hesitation. "I'm up against some thug by the name of Gitmo."

After a brief, dead silence came a voice. "Gitmo? Gitmo Debt? GD? THE Gitmo Debt?"

It sounded as though whoever this was, was very familiar with Gitmo. To my relief, he seemed somewhat amused. By the way he sarcastically responded, I could tell there was a lot more behind this that I needed to know.

"Yeah," I said. "He's coming after my little business. But why he's picking on me, I'll never know. At any rate, he's going to be a big problem for me."

"Well . . . you've got the right guy. I'm your trainer." Kanketa's voice was confident and deliberate.

"What qualifies you to train me against Gitmo?" I challenged. "You don't know anything about my business."

He had a quick comeback. "What kind of car do you drive?"

"A 2016 Chevy Malibu."

"Could you trust that I can get into your car right now and drive it to town and back?"

"That's a no-brainer. Well, of course, you probably can."

"But why would you ever trust this? I've never driven a 2016 Chevy Malibu. Could you trust that you can drive in the Indy 500?"

I didn't know where he was going with this. I said nothing.

"Since the day the idea of the invention of business, its layouts have been generally the same; the basic functions are the same, and the rules of the road are all the same. Driving a car isn't just moving a machine. Driving creates an experience. And driving a business isn't just moving a product or service. It creates an experience. Driving is learning to choose the quickest, the safest, and the most convenient route for the situation." There was no hesitance in Mr. Kanketa's sentences. He spoke confidently.

"I've invested many years, gaining experience and learning to create solutions with my skills along the way. And now, I'm a race car driver. For decades, I've driven many different kinds of businesses, of every size, type, shape, description, and color. I've studied, honed, and mastered my business skills. While you might have driven a few tracks, I've driven many, many hundreds. You've learned defensive driving from a few mistakes. I've learned from many, many hundreds. Today, you're in a new, unfamiliar town and you need to get to an address quickly. I know the quickest and safest route. I've earned the right to be your driver, your trainer."

"I get your point."

After a brief silence, he commented, "I've boxed in the ring with Gitmo numerous times."

"Did you win?"

"Not at first. It took a while to learn his conniving strategies and moves. Gradually, I discovered his weaknesses and limitations. With each match, winning became easier and easier. I still don't always win every round. I just never lose a match."

I appreciated and frankly enjoyed Kanketa's uncompromising candor. I was growing less apprehensive and a little more relieved with every word that rolled off his tongue. It was obvious that Kanketa had developed sharp listening skills, and it was equally evident that he understood what I was saying. I found myself doing all the selling. The convincing to have him as my trainer came straight from me. I was answering my own questions and coming to my own conclusions. Clearly, I was engaged in conversation with someone of marked experience. In our short phone exchange, it was plain to hear that Mr. Kanketa was well-qualified to train—and certainly over-qualified to train—a beginner like me.

"I want you to know that I'm on a short leash," I warned. "Gitmo is here, and has scheduled a Fight Night. I don't have much time to get in shape." Kanketa quoted me a ten-week training package. I had little choice but to accept before all my debts would completely ruin me.

"Let's just say I'm interested. Do you have references?"

Kanketa wasn't hiding a thing. I was quick to discover that providing me with his testimonials would be nothing more than a courteous professional gesture on his part. Yet, he graciously accepted my request.

"How many references do you want?"

A low-growl hmmm came from my hoarse throat, but I didn't really answer him. It was clear that I didn't care about his references. He probably sensed that I was somewhat desperate, and he knew I had already bought his whole package lock, stock, and barrel. He could name his price. He did. We settled on his ten-week training program.

"Over the years, I've fought long and hard with old Gitmo," he proceeded. "After many years in my own businesses, I learned how to counter his moves. There's not much you can tell me about ol' Gitmo Debt that I don't already know, or haven't experienced firsthand. But as trainers go, I can't make you a champ in the first round. Your wins are going to hopefully come over seven or eight rounds. I just won't let you stretch yourself out to the full twelve. As long as you are already in the match, you'll have to fight your way out. The questions become, how hard are you willing to train, and how fast can you make this go with the least injury—and the biggest prize?"

We continued on the phone for a few more minutes and I took his information.

Mr. Kanketa agreed to locate a gym in the area. We scheduled training two nights a week for the next ten weeks.

CHAPTER 3

THE 9Ms OF BUSINESS BOXING

The Interview

On the following Tuesday, I had my first meeting. It wasn't really a training session, but rather a "getting-to-know-ya" interview.

At 6:30 p.m., after a full day of work, I walked out into a balmy evening with a breathtaking golden sunset. I went directly from the office to meet Mr. Kanketa at the gym. I was my usual prompt self. Within fifteen minutes, I met him in the lobby with my gym bag in hand.

My hunch was right. Mr. Kanketa was just as I had envisioned him.

My eyes scanned him from head to toe. He was a short, balding Asian man with thick, black, horn-rimmed glasses. A thinning, well-groomed goatee harbored the smooth skin on his face. He was wearing a dark-blue polo shirt that hung loosely over his firm figure. It complemented his crisp, neatly pressed khaki pants. He wore a tightly woven straw fedora with a small red feather that was tucked into a colorful chartreuse hatband. His polished, beige leather loafers were a nice touch. Clearly, Kanketa was in a class all his own.

I suspected we would do more talking than swinging punches in our first get-together. I realized after I suited up that it was pointless.

We didn't go directly to the ring, but reconvened in the lobby. He invited me to sit in a rickety old lobby chair. His demeanor firmly communicated that I was about to be thoroughly interrogated.

"So . . . how's business? Up? Down? In between?" he began. His question was a pleasant distraction from my worry-filled day. He was already on the clock, and I was obligated to answer.

"It's up overall. Orders are steady. Referrals are good. No complaints so far."

"So, tell me. What's the good news?" he inquired. "What do you like about your business?"

I didn't know this guy from Adam. I could have been talking to anyone. Yet, somehow, he had a charming way of disarming me and putting me at ease. It might have been the way he demonstrated his listening skills.

He came across concerned, respectful, and caring. He certainly wasn't salesy. That's what I immediately liked about him. I found him refreshing. I didn't resist or try to control the conversation. I just let him lead.

"I enjoy the freedom of setting my own schedule, and controlling the outcome of my decisions without having to answer to anyone. I have three great employees and I'm looking around for a fourth. We've been in business for about twenty months now, and it's starting to actually feel like a business. I used to work from home, but recently we moved into a small office on Westbury Street."

"So, tell me . . ." he said. "If you could improve just one thing right now about your business, what would it be?"

"Cash flow. Definitely, cash flow. My customers aren't paying as fast as I need. They seem to completely ignore my payment terms, and they are steering the ship, just because they can."

Kanketa stopped to validate me. "No worries. You're not alone. I hear this from a lot of business owners. It seems to be the flavor of the day."

"Why do you think Gitmo is hanging around me all of a sudden?" I writhed.

"He sees an opportunity to push you to your knees if you run out of cash. Destroying your business is his sole mission."

I wasn't surprised at his comment. I nodded in agreement.

After a brief moment of contemplative silence, he spoke up. "So, what do you think it will take to fix your cash flow problem?"

"Probably a reasonable line of credit."

Mr. Kanketa fired his questions non-stop. "How is this cash flow issue impacting your business?"

"We can't take on the new customers that I'd like. We're in a holding pattern for orders from our two biggest clients that are critical to our growth. If we don't grow now, we'll slide backward."

"How is the cash flow problem affecting you personally?"

I seemed to be keeping pace with Kanketa's line of questioning. "Needless to say, I'm stressed. Constantly worrying about bills. Payroll keeps me up at night. I can't say my sleeping habits are the best. In fact, they're closer to non-existent. I'm putting our family through purgatory."

"What have you done so far to tackle this problem?"

Just then I realized that I hardly ever stop long enough to hear myself talk. At this point, I was learning a whole lot from my own words that seemed to tumble freely from my lips.

"Those darn banks. I keeping applying here and there. I actually need a fifty-grand line of credit. The banks won't give me fifty bucks. I fill out their damn applications over and over to no avail. Those bankers just can't see the big picture."

There was no delay between Kanketa's questions. "Why now?" he asked. "It sounds like you've had this problem for quite a while. Is cash flow your biggest priority at the moment? Can you put this problem off until a later time? Maybe a few months from now? Can this wait?"

I choked in dismay. "Not a minute more. I'll lose big opportunities that are staring me in the face right now. I'll lose them to my competitors. This can't be put off any longer."

He pondered. "So . . . what's stopping you from solving your cash problem?"

"Mr. Kanketa, I'll be frank. I keep saying that I need the line of credit I need. But, even if I had the money, my business needs organization. I know how to create a product in my business. I just don't know where to go from there. Yes, I've owned my business for a while, but running it successfully alludes me. It all remains a mystery."

Mr. Kanketa's upper right lip curled into a smile. "So, I'm hearing that the real root cause of the problem is that you need some management skills along with the cash."

Right there and then, he cornered me. I was caught dead in my tracks. If Mr. Kanketa was attempting to sell me, it wasn't obvious.

In fact, I didn't recall a single declarative sentence during his interview. He simply asked me questions. By my count, there were seven questions in all. Even though the interview was going well and he was listening intently, I must admit that my mind drifted in and out between the conversation and the long list of payables that confronted me at work. The distraction kept me restless. I was having difficulty focusing on our discussion.

"I'd like to make a request," I interrupted. "Can we get on with the training?"

"Your training started when you showed up," he pointed out.

Mr. Kanketa reached into his pocket and pulled out a tightly folded paper. As he peeled back the corners, he announced his first instruction.

"This will be your training agenda. Your mission, should you choose to accept it, is to memorize every word on this paper. Over the coming weeks we will cover different points at every session until you have them down cold."

I enthusiastically vowed that I would memorize the agenda and after a quick glance, I tucked the paper in the pocket of my gym shorts.

TRAINING AGENDA

Strength Training, Your Manpower

Most Trusted Partners, Your MTP

The Ring, Your "Milieu" (Work Space)

The Correct Position, Your Mind-set

Hand Wraps, Your Materials

Clubs and Dumbbells, Your Machines

Punching The Bag, Your Methods

Scoring, Your Measurements

Diet and Nutrition, Money Management

The tone of our conversation shifted, but I could see that he wasn't going to start without answers to more questions. Our interview was over for the moment. We adjourned.

I must admit, I left the gym with a mix of confusion and relief.

Session 1:
Manpower, MTP, Milieu

Thursday couldn't come soon enough. The first training session was underway. When he walked in, I was standing there in my attire. My diligence didn't seem to impress him. He dove right into the topic of the day.

"Let's talk about your strength. Why do you think you can beat Gitmo Debt?"

"I'm strong, I'm determined, and I'm angry as hell," I retorted. That was one answer I was sure of. I pressed on.

"In just the short period of time that I've had my business, I've struggled and scraped, been bruised, beaten, and bullied, and I've been pulled through the wringer and out the other end. So far, my business has been no picnic. I definitely pass the passion test."

Mr. Kanketa smiled again. "Not quite enough," he said. "I had a good trainer once. Lenny used to tell me to stay smart, stay humble, and stay hungry. Those were good words to live by. That philosophy kept me strong, focused, and on track.

This time, he tossed some oblique ones at me that I hardly expected.

"Assuming that you are as strong as you say, do you have the desire to grow?"

I was perplexed. Out of the gate, it was a puzzling question. "Of course I want to grow. Doesn't everybody?"

His questions weren't just rhetoric. "If you were to pose this question to a thousand business owners, almost all of them would tell you explicitly that they want to grow their business. What does growth mean to you?"

"I used to think that growth was getting more from doing more of what I am good at. Recently, my definition has widened. It used to be about I and me and what I like to do. Now I see growth as about having a bigger impact, the difference I can make for others, and hopefully in the long-term, some financial reward for my family. When I talk about growth these days, I consider long-term as well as short-term." I thought my answer was admirable. He was less impressed.

"Very few business owners actually want to grow. They love the fight. The sense of accomplishment. But when they go up against the real tough contenders, they get weak in the knees. When it comes right down to it, many aren't really in love with their business at all. They can't see making it their life's calling. It just beats the employment alternative. Having a business these days and calling yourself CEO is cool and trendy, and it contributes to ego-boosting conversation at parties. That is why most businesses rarely get beyond the kitchen table. They aren't really willing to do what it takes."

Strength Training: Manpower

He saw the determination on my face. His second question followed without hesitation. "Do you have the will to change?" His face was stern.

While the answer seemed rudimentary, it did take a little thought. Possibilities flashed through my mind. What will be asked of me?

Will I really be able to change? How much change? A little? A lot? How soon? Could I change a little mannerism, or must I break my lousy ingrained habits from years of guesswork? Nonetheless, I was still compelled to show my commitment to Mr. K.

"Yes, of course I am willing to make changes," I said with resolve.

"That's not what I asked. Many business owners are willing to have successful businesses, but they lack the will to do what it takes to create one. Your will is your biggest strength," he continued. "It is your Manpower. But, like strengthening a muscle, your willpower must be constantly exercised. Willpower combines your intention with your certainty and purpose to create action. This is when you are able to produce a predictable result with minimal wasted effort. So I ask once again, do you have the will to make necessary changes?"

His complex statement was a bit difficult to grasp at first. It sprang out of context from our everyday, down-to-earth conversation, yet it couldn't have been more eloquently delivered. There wasn't a word out of place or anything I would have changed. Still, it took a few moments to understand. Then, the meaning came to me.

"Yes, I believe that I have the willpower."

His third question followed closely behind. "Good. So, now tell me. Are you playing to win, or just playing?"

This time, I might have come off sounding a bit irritated and defiant. "I'm playing to win. That's it. Winning is everything to me." He knew I was being spunky. He was testing my stamina.

"And how does your idea of growth change your approach to growing?" he asked. "After all, you took your business from your basement to the street."

I was steadfast in my reply. "Right now, I'm using my instincts. I know there are tools to grow. I just don't know what they are or where to find them."

Most Trusted Partners: MTP

Mr. Kanketa's next question was straightforward and unsuspecting.

"Do you trust me?"

"Mr. K., we wouldn't be here right now if I didn't trust you implicitly."

"Do you trust what I say?"

Again, I was confused, but responded politely, "Yes, I trust what you say."

"Magnificent. Because I'm going to ask you to hang your business experiences up at the door. This training will not be comfortable, and the success of your match with Gitmo Debt will be completely reliant upon your ability to put your complete faith in me and in my process. This means that I must know what you are thinking, doing, and feeling at all times."

I wasn't there to sharpen my argument skills. In that moment, he gained full control of my attention.

"Everything I tell you to do comes with its own set of conditions and requirements. We won't move forward until I am sure that you understand what I'm saying, you agree with it, and you see the personal benefit to you. All three must be in place or my training comes to a screeching halt. I want you to understand that I have your best interest in mind. And finally, I must insist on three values. They have to be present at all times. It will be the air that you will breathe during our training. A, I, R. Accountability. Integrity. Respect."

I couldn't help but admire his insistence on values. He picked three of my best.

"Accountability requires your willingness to accept responsibility for your actions without blaming anything or anyone outside of yourself. Integrity is simply saying what you do, doing what you say, and helping others along the way. Respect always considers me as having abilities, qualities, achievements, and experiences that you do not have. I am your authority in this training. Without these in place, we can't move forward. I am your MTP, your most trusted partner."

I didn't waiver with his demands. "I'm in."

"Excellent. Then, let's talk about the ring."

The Ring: "Milieu" (Work Space)

Kanketa motioned me to the main doorway of the gym. He exuded stability and a relentless conviction to make me a business champion. His unfaltering manner bolstered my confidence exponentially. I felt comfortable. I was in good hands.

The humid practice room gave off a slight musty odor. The bright spotlights added a good fifteen degrees to the already-warm center ring. Indubitably, it was a practice ring.

"This is where you will live. Everything you do will only be counted in the ring. You will win in the ring, or you will lose in the ring. If you are to win the match, you must respect every inch of the mat."

"Respect the ring?"

Kanketa channeled my thoughts.

"Many fighters do not respect the ring. They don't see their business as an everyday opportunity to improve. Then, they wonder why they lose. They look at their business as a place to get work done. They don't see the waste. They overlook the thousands of inches of opportunity to grow without adding more expense."

Then, Mr. Kanketa led me to the center of the ring and pointed. There laid a damp towel that someone left. He showed me the frayed ropes and the indented plastic mat.

"Without question, this is a practice gym, but winning should be logical, predictable, and repeatable, based on everything you must be able to count on," he pointed out. "If you constantly practice under poor conditions that are less than you might expect in the professional ring, you will develop sloppy, wasteful habits. Nothing will be predictable because you can't rely on good conditions. So, you will naturally and instinctively punch harder and exert more energy than you would normally need to, because you have experienced the ring differently. These are how bad habits are developed. Your business is your boxing ring. It must have a degree of built-in reliability, predictability, and safety. Poor equipment and a disorganized, poorly maintained ring won't offer you the reliability you will need to count on."

Kanketa walked to the water cooler nearby. I remained stationary, motionless.

"Your business is your 'Milieu.' It is the work space that you must master. You must completely and assuredly own it, every foot, from the front door to the back door and every micro-inch of space in between, with everything that it takes. I'm even talking about those virtual inches of memory in your computers. Whether your fighting ring is in your home, in your computer, or in an outside office, it is your milieu, your work space. It must always remain in top condition."

He reached for a small paper cup on the water cooler and held it under the tap. His voice was intermittent as it competed with the repeated rhythm of the loud gurgles from the water as it cleared the spout. Between sips, he spoke in an authoritative tone.

"If you are to be a lean, clean, fighting machine that wins rounds and continues to win matches predictably, you must organize your business for reliability and standardization. This will demand an optimized work space that requires your commitment and the commitment of everyone in your company. Potential business problems must be easily and quickly identified. In your work space, you must be able to quickly and efficiently improve the quality and output of your processes and products by removing waste and error. Your ring must be clean of debris, with no defective or accumulated items that are outdated or unnecessary. Timing will always be crucial to your success. You should never have to search for anything, such as hand wraps, antiseptics, and medical supplies.

Mike Wolf

Everything you need must always be on hand and within reach when you need it. Your ring should be kept spotless at all times and fit for use, ready for the bell."

He crumpled the paper cup and tossed it in the wastebasket nearby.

"This leads me to another point—standardization. You don't go into the ring swinging wildly in hopes of hitting something. There is a fixed position, a protective stance, left glove up, right foot ahead of left, to ensure that every swing has a defined, specific, measurable, achievable, reachable target. These are standards that are proven to work over centuries of boxing. The most famous boxers have written volumes about them and have committed their writings to professional training libraries."

As he talked, I mentally walked through my office. Honestly, this must have been the very first time I was internally quiet enough to do that. It was in that moment I realized how disorganized we were. After nearly two years of operating my company, I was only at the starting line with organization. I could see all of the waste. It wasn't just wasted materials or space. There was so much wasted time, and I had no idea how to count it, measure it, track it, or control it. My office would be a field day for Gitmo Debt.

"Manpower, MTP, and Milieu; Manpower are your strengths, MTP are your most trusted partnerships, and Milieu is your efficient work space. All businesses have these basic resources in their quiver, but few are aware of their vital importance or use them with any degree of consistency or effectiveness. These are the first three of your nine resources. Without balance and a plan for each, your business will soon dwarf, with little hope for growth."

I was appreciative and thanked him for his perspective. After ninety minutes, we disbanded and agreed to resume on Thursday at the same time. I never did throw my first punch.

Session 2:
Mind-set, Materials, Machines

In Thursday's session, there wasn't a wasted minute. Mr. Kanketa began with a quick review of Manpower, MTP, and Milieu. I must say, I surprised myself. I was able to concisely recite their definitions and values. I didn't skip a beat.

Kanketa complimented me for my effort.

"Today we will home in on the next three resources: your Mind-set, Materials, and Machines. I will begin with mind-set as the single, most crucial attribute in the world of business."

Mr. K. and I were on the same page with the criticality of mind-set. However, when he began to share his viewpoint, his definitions put me in my own swim lane. Mind-set was much more to him than a motivational speech about maintaining a positive attitude.

The Correct Position: Mind-set

"Mind-set is the nutrition of the soul. It's also the breeding ground for Gitmo's strength. Your biggest fight will not be Gitmo. It will be the fight in your head. You will be fighting your **F**-ears, your **A**-ssumptions, your **I**-nterpretations, and your **L**-imiting beliefs about your business. These four horsemen spell FAIL. This is the acronym for business owners who allow interruption and distraction from their vision, mission, and true purpose. Your undying attitude

27

must be to constantly inspire everyone in your audience. It's up to you to set the stage. Your Mind-set resource is the alignment of your attitudes with the attitudes of your team members toward a singleness of purpose. Lead yourself and inspire others. What is it that is interrupting and holding you back from having everything in your business exactly the way you want it? Don't tell me it's cash flow. It goes much deeper than money."

I couldn't think of the answer. No one had ever asked me that before.

"You're right," I admitted. "Over the last few months, I was definitely moping and being short with everyone. I recently noticed that my employees were clamming up. I couldn't prove it, but it felt like everyone was saying to themselves, 'I'll just shut my mouth and do my job.' My lousy attitude spread across my company. The employees aren't volunteering suggestions like they used to. They are keeping to themselves. I guess I've generated some poor morale."

Kanketa spoke softly, with understanding. "No right or wrong here. No judgements. Just choices and consequences." He was definitely following his own agenda. It had solid continuity and flow.

"People are in their own businesses for untold reasons. There are those in business because they want to do what they love and share it with others. There are the team players who are entering a second phase of their careers, and took a risk by starting their own businesses. There are the passionately confident risk-takers who are born to be business owners. They enjoy choosing their own path and are very passionate about their life's work. Then come the traditional types, who inherited their status as small business owners from a family member or a friend. They are working in the business doing what Dad wanted and expected."

I interrupted. "I knew how to do something well, and thought I could do it better than anyone else. I went into business to have more time for myself. Unfortunately, I didn't have any real training. Over time, the business grew. And now, I don't have the training or the skills to keep up with it."

"You fall into the category of the self-motivated. They start their own business for the opportunity to get what they most value— control over their schedules and hours. It's all over the board. I've observed over the years that women are more likely than men to say they started their business for flexible hours. The visionaries begin their business because they see an opportunity and want to capitalize on it. Men, more likely than women, say they started their business because they believed they could do it better than their competitors, and are more likely to say they always knew they would someday own their own business. Then there are those 'experienced' business professionals who leave their profitable corporate life, usually unsatisfying day jobs, for one reason—to become their own boss. More than half of all those I've known said they always wanted to work for themselves and not have a boss."

I concurred with Mr. Kanketa's experiences. "So, it's all about mind-set?"

"Absolutely. Your first order of business is to discover who you really are. You must get to the answer of why you are in business. How do you help? Whom do help? What problems do you solve? Are you all in, half in, or just hugging the Gatorade cooler and waving at your momma? Do you plan to make your business a hobby or are you going to move into the professional ring?"

I couldn't tell if he was serious. "Hobby? What's that supposed to mean?"

"A hobbyist has an idea about something that could be saleable. It could be cookies at a fair. It could be the next Google. Hobby doesn't imply lesser value of an idea, but it is still categorized as a hobby because a hobbyist is technically operating in bankruptcy."

"Bankruptcy?" I started to feel like I was under attack. I was somewhat offended by his insinuation of bankruptcy and found myself quite on the defensive.

"Today my small business might be new, but it is debt-free, and with all of its problems and foibles, it still kicks out a comfortable living. Actually, after my first two years, I'm doing just fine. My business is hardly bankrupt. In fact, I don't even know why Gitmo is bothering with my debt-free company."

"My dear friend, I am over-delighted to hear that your business is working so well for you. By the strictest definition and standards, if your business is depositing less than $50,000 a year, you are a hobby. A few fairs a year, a farmer's market, a trade show or two, and you've got a hobby. But if you expect more from it, you are almost guaranteed to have less than $1.00 of income to pay for every $1.00 of debt in hobby mode. In the professional business ring, your hobby is operating in bankruptcy. You just haven't filed for bankruptcy, and might never do so."

"We sell $25,000 a month on the average. We are no longer a hobby," I mumbled.

He could see that I was struggling to understand. His teaching style was uniquely explicit. He went on.

"Gitmo is coming at you because he knows there is no such thing as debt-free. If, at any minute, you decided to abruptly stop your business, you might have cash in the bank to pay all outstanding debts. However, you would owe someone, somewhere, the balance of something; an unpaid rent balance, an unpaid phone bill, an unpaid cost of a product or service. There's always close-out expenses to cease business operations that might not have been considered. No one in their right mind—not Buffett, not Gates, no one—pre-pays every possible expense of their company and can simply stop the business without paying something to someone. Before you scream from the rooftops that none of this applies to you, consider that in nearly all 'debt-free' small businesses that I've ever trained, almost none have had less than 20 percent unrecognized, unrecorded, and unreported debts. I often find this number to be closer to percent"

"I'm not sure what debts you are talking about," I sputtered. "I agree that a hobbyist is anyone who is standing outside the ring with an idea, a concept, but . . ."

Kanketa completed my sentence. "Yes . . . and they might even have an LLC with an EIN number, and they might be with or without a business plan. They just haven't really fully stepped all in to the ring yet."

"Well, rest assured, Mr. Kanketa. I'm not a hobbyist in my business."

"A person behind the wheel of a car doesn't get to say that they are qualified to drive. Only a driver's license tells that you are qualified. The hobbyist doesn't get to say whether he or she has a hobby. The rules, and nothing else, define the hobbyist."

Mr. Kanketa was starting to make some real sense. He was proving to be the right trainer for the right fight.

Hand Wraps, Your Materials

"It's time to put on some protective wrapping around your business," Mr. K. insisted. He pulled my hands toward him and began to wrap them with stretch wrap from a thick roll on the corner of the mat.

"It's one thing to know how to do the work. It's quite another to be able to do it. You will need what you need when you need it— supplies on hand. This will take teamwork with your MTPs. You will need cooperation and collaboration with key suppliers; not just anyone who has supplies available. These are a few of the very best people you can find, who go beyond the call of duty to help you no matter what. They have your best interest in mind and want you to succeed. They constantly attack themselves with ways to create continuous improvement. They work on standardization and organization. They bring your materials to you on target, on budget, and on time, error-free. They are only a few. Only the best."

"I don't think materials apply to my business. We don't buy materials. You're thinking about a construction or manufacturing business. We are a consulting service. Our consulting firm doesn't have supplies."

Kanketa smirked and looked down to inspect his wrapping.

"Every business on the planet has costs related to a job, no matter how seemingly insignificant. A restaurant has raw food supplies and sauces, a barbershop has combs and creams, an insurance agent has proposal covers, even a non-profit, a church, has church bulletins."

"I can't think of what supplies we would have in our business. We just sell time!" I exclaimed.

"At one time or other, you might have heard of the term 'variable cost.' A variable cost is often called Cost of Goods Sold. These are expenses that you only have if you have a job. This is the total amount that it costs to produce and sell a product or service. If you have twenty jobs, each job has its own list of cost of goods sold, or variable costs, related to each specific order. Supplies, materials, and job-related expenses, equipment rentals, and shipping specifically for the job are all variable costs. If you do not have the work, there are no variable costs to pay."

"I still don't see how this applies to my business," I refuted.

"Would you need boxing gloves if you didn't have a match?"

"No, I wouldn't."

"Exactly. Boxing gloves are a variable cost. And, would you need a trainer if you weren't planning to box?"

"Nope."

Kanketa replied sharply, "Certainly not. I am a variable cost." He didn't allow room for a comment. "And in your business, have you ever contracted outside help?"

"Oh yeah, when we get real busy and can't do the work ourselves—"

He stopped me. "There is a variable cost. Outside contract labor services that you hire to do a job." He went on. "And did you ever buy proposal covers?"

"All the time," I answered.

"There's a variable cost. And do you ever use Federal Express? If you didn't have the job, you wouldn't need Federal Express, would you?"

I was starting to catch on. I threw the idea forward. "So, then, my cost of goods sold includes sales commissions and finder fees that I would pay to anyone outside of our company. I wouldn't pay commission if we didn't have the job."

"Absolutely," he confirmed.

"I wouldn't pay sales tax if we didn't have the job."

"Right again. As you can see, there are many types of variable costs of goods sold that are directly related to specific jobs that you do. You might have many jobs, but each job has its own one-time variable costs. You only have cost of goods if you have a job."

That was one point of clarity that I never counted on. My limited ideas got the best of me.

"So . . . in the consulting arena, I should line up my key outside suppliers and invite them to be part of my business process?"

"Your key suppliers should partner with you and be willing to learn your business and your processes. They should monitor your system and constantly offer suggestions for improvement. Otherwise, they are just a bunch of order-taking telemarketers."

Clubs and Dumbbells: The Machines

Kanketa's teaching approach was refreshing. But I was becoming impatient; I'd had enough talk. I was beyond anxious to start my physical training. With my wrapped hands I approached the bag, ready to hit. Kanketa grabbed my wrist and blocked the punch. Then he handed me two Indian clubs of five pounds each.

"Every morning, I want you to swing these clubs in a windmill circular motion for fifteen minutes. You need to build strength in your wrists. Then, go to dumbbells in a slower motion. You must loosen your shoulders. Once you crawl into the professional business boxing ring, it will be easier to understand why you must build strength into your business practices. They have little or no value to anyone except you. For the last two years you have been using the loosened-up rules for dipping your toe in the water that work in a startup company. Today those timid approaches no longer apply. When you are all in instead of toe in, you will want to keep loose and limber for the next level of performance."

"What are you driving at?" I queried.

"Your business machines will evolve along with your business demands."

I had not thought of business machines in my company like he was about to explain.

"The machines in your business aren't necessarily for the formation or assembly of products. They are any machines to produce and deliver your work more efficiently. They are computers, cell phones, fax machines, a postage machine, even a car. Given this definition, what machines will you need to win the Debt fight?" It was a new perspective. I wasn't ready for it.

"I guess I will have to look over my payables list to see what I need in the way of machines. I will most likely need specific USB storage sticks for one of our jobs. I will need to rent some measuring and testing equipment for one of our projects. I will also need an iPad for remote Skyping. And an extra car besides my own that is strictly used for visiting customers. Guess there are more machines in the picture than I thought."

He cocked his fedora on his head and gave me a wide smile. "You might find your way around them. But actively working with these clubs and dumbbells will give you efficiency to execute faster slugs." He nodded.

"Mind-set, materials, machines. That should wrap it up for tonight," he decided.

I agreed. It was a very full night.

Session 3: Punching The Bag:
Measurements, Methods, and Money

Another week went by.

On Tuesday, we were already on session three and I hadn't touched a punching bag or even been in the ring yet. I was getting hives from the stress of no physical training. It was all good stuff, but what in the hell was Kanketa thinking?

"You are my sunshine, my only sunshine. You make me happeeeee when skies are gray," I chanted in a low tone.

"What are you singing?" Kanketa asked.

"My mother always made me sing 'You are my Sunshine' whenever I got nervous or afraid. It always soothed me in tough times. Right now, I'm apprehensive, and downright horrified. Do you happen to recall who I'm up against in a couple of weeks? I'm fighting for my business life!"

Kanketa completely ignored my jabbering. "Your mother was wise to have you do that," he pointed out. "Everyone needs a relief trigger. Something that takes your mind to a higher ground."

Mr. Kanketa stood and watched as I swung the clubs for just shy of fifteen minutes. It was harder than I thought. Hooray! He finally planted the punching bag in front of my face.

"A punching bag is basic to your understanding of boxing. There are three kinds of bags, each with different weights," he explained. "You are going to find various levels of resistance in your business, and I will train you to give punches to all of them."

I perked up and gave Mr. Kanketa my full attention. I was starting to learn something of value and I didn't want to miss a trick.

"Rule one in boxing: never punch at a motionless bag. If a business debt is the lowest negotiated level that you can get to without pissing off a good supplier, leave it alone. Stop trying to negotiate further. You will only make the supplier fight you harder. They don't get mad. They get even."

"Got it."

"Make it a win-win. Allow your suppliers to breath. Allow them to make money too. If you don't, they won't be there when you need them. Once you've hit their bottom line of tolerance, leave it alone.

"And rule number two: never hit the bag as it is coming toward you. Chances are excellent that you'll dislocate your wrist. Catch it as it swings away from you. Your business is no different. Don't try to fix debt problems without full, accurate information and understanding. Let the suppliers come at you with all the facts first. Allow yourself to understand the complete picture before trying to reactively resolve the issue. These two basic rules are critical to your position in the ring.

"Your position point is called D-T-I. It is the most important number in your business."

"D-T-I? What about profit?" I interjected. "I thought profit was the most important number in my business."

Mr. Kanketa was quick to correct me. "No. Profit is not the most important number in your business. D-T-I is far more telling. D-T-I is your fight score. It is the number that will determine whether you are succeeding or failing in each round. D-T-I, and only D-T-I, is the first, and biggest reason why all those small businesses lose to Gitmo Debt. They use profit as their gauge. They weren't trained correctly."

Scoring: The D-T-I Measurements

"What does D-T-I stand for?" I pleaded to know.

Mr. Kanketa went on. "D-T-I is your ratio of Debt to Income, the relationship of all of your debts to all of the income you have to pay off those debts. In other words, it's the amount of money you have to work with to run your business at any given moment after all your debts have been paid. Your income minus your debt will always tell you whether you are winning or losing on a moment-to-moment basis. Your net profit is part of the money left over, but so are your salaries and non-people costs. It is a far better bet to monitor your D-T-I score than the typical end of the month 'profit' figure that you might see at the bottom of your Profit and Loss Statement.

"Your D-T-I score is simple math. It is the total of all your income divided by the total of all your debts. This is where we will begin in our training. But there is much to learn about income and debt, and it's not what you might think."

I didn't want to interrupt Mr. Kanketa, but this money talk gave me the heebie-jeebies. I was never much good with numbers. I failed fifth-grade arithmetic. By the way he was talking, it was beginning to sound like I would have to be some sort of math genius to run my business. I was generally doing okay without D-T-I. And now I was getting uncomfortable. Besides, it sounded like more work, and more work was not what I was training for. He detected my anxiety and attempted to put me at ease.

"Simple addition, subtraction, multiplication, and division is all you will never need to run your business. Nothing more," he said. "Knowing your D-T-I score is as important to your business as any of the products or services you are producing."

D-T-I is the total of all your income divided by the total of all debt items.

"Once you have a total of all of your income and a total of all your debts, you will divide the income by the debt to get your D-T-I number. The more accurately you record your income and debt items, the more accurate and quickly you can learn to throw the D-T-I punch. The goal is to get your D-T-I up as high as possible. The higher the D-T-I, the safer, the healthier, the more profitable, and the more valuable your business will be."

He went to a nearby blackboard and picked up some chalk.

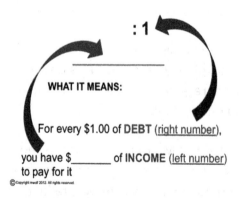

: 1

WHAT IT MEANS:

For every $1.00 of DEBT (right number),
you have $_____ of INCOME (left number)
to pay for it

"D-T-I measurements are displayed in dollar ranges. The amount of income is on the left. The right side shows one dollar of debt that is owed. For every $1.00 of debt, which is the number on the right, you have the income number on the left to pay for it. Let me give you an example."

He started scribbling on a nearby whiteboard. His writing was unusually even and legible.

"Let's say you have total debts of $80,000 and income of $100,000. The 100 divided by 80 gives you your D-T-I of $1.25 to $1. This is your debt-to-income ratio . . . your D-T-I.

"Your total income minus your total debt is more appropriately your NET income, the money that finally falls into the net that your company can operate with at any single moment, including your profit. Missing or overlooking any debt or income item can cause your D-T-I to be inaccurate, and that could cost you a lot of wasted time and money, and even hold up or stop a bank from lending to you. Always be sure to get the most accurate numbers."

Just More Work?

I recoiled. "Excuse me, Mr. K., but I've been doing just fine without ever once calculating or monitoring my D-T-I score. Is D-T-I just more work that I don't want?"

"Just fine? Is all your stress, the mystery you refer to and the guesswork with no reliable, predictable, repeatable, sustainable performance results what you call 'just fine'?"

He let me off the hook. "Your D-T-I is a wonderful forecasting tool that will forewarn you of any oncoming, unforeseen, uncontrollable factors that could, and often do, happen without warning. When you are caught off guard, it might be too late to recover. That is when you will immediately need money and your recovery options quickly. Your D-T-I score will alert you ahead of time, and tell the bank how much they can loan you, and how fast. Be prepared to never expect more for your business than your D-T-I score is able to give you. Keep in mind that it is your D-T-I, not your bank, that determines the value and health of your business."

I couldn't help being impressed with Mr. Kanketa's perspective. "Mr. Kanketa . . . it always stumped me why those multi-billion-dollar empires go bankrupt, with their floors and teams of the brightest minds in the business."

He turned to me with a smirk. "Many of those six-figure MBA financial analysts, consultants, and accountants from the most highly acclaimed business schools in the country had the right ladder leaning against the wrong wall. My experience tells me that they misjudged the actual performance of their companies because they were using ticket sales to make in-the-ring decisions when all along they needed a playbook. This explains why, in nearly all cases, they failed miserably while their profits were over the top—more often than not, the highest in their company's history."

Bankrupt (DTI under 1.10:1)
THESE COMPANIES COULD NOT BORROW
ENOUGH MONEY TO AVOID BANKRUPTCY.

DTI DISCOVERED
TOO LATE. NO PLAN!

MOST BUSINESSES

INCORRECTLY STATE
OR OVERLOOK
**AT LEAST 4 DTI
ITEMS ...**

"I get it, I get it, Mr. Kanketa. So, they were using their huge profits to pay off even bigger debts. It was a debt problem, not a lack of profit problem."

The big smile that filled his face revealed that he was being richly rewarded for his teaching.

I was committed to become an expert. We retired the evening with a recap of my nine resources; Manpower, MTP, Milieu, Mind-set, Materials, Machines, Methods, Measurements, and Money.

Admittedly, tonight's session was very helpful. It gave me a good look at myself from thirty thousand feet through the lens of the business world.

We shook hands and left on a high note.

CHAPTER 4

12 DEBTS. "THE DIRTY DOZEN"

Session 4: Twelve Debts that can put a Business out of Business

Once again, Thursday couldn't come quickly enough. I was so caught up in unfinished paperwork I had to actively make a conscious decision to put it off. I drove like a maniac directly to the gym. I might have missed a red light in my hurry. Not quite sure.

I was on time, however. Promptness was one of my more redeeming qualities. Mr. Kanketa met me at the door. We started the session with a few minutes of idle chat. He shifted his body position in his chair and angled his fedora to the left. He was undeniably ready for business. Kanketa led the conversation.

"Over the years, I've watched Gitmo Debt closely He always uses the same dirty dozen punches. I promised to teach them to you, and I always keep my promises. Tell me about your business debts. Who do you owe money to?

"We owe money to our suppliers."

"Most businesses do. But suppliers are just one of twelve kinds of debt," he said. He threw me a curveball.

"There are twelve debts that can put a business out of business."

"Really? Twelve? Well, then, I'm a little confused. I always called debt something that I owed or that I'm bound to pay or perform."

Mr. Kanketa's eyes looked firmly into mine. "Partially true. Said a better way, a debt is a liability or obligation to pay something. But your business has debts to suppliers, employees, customers, banks, the government, friends, and family, and even to you as the owner that are real but you don't see them as payable."

I hadn't considered this list.

"We're going to talk about them in the order of their appearance, but not necessarily in the order of their importance."

Whenever Kanketa got enthused about an idea, his voice would escalate and he would build into a windup. He just did.

"Before you spend all of your income money, you will need to take a hard, cold, no-kidding look at everything you owe. Some things on the debt list might throw you. To keep things simple, all business debts are summed up in three categories; debts to employees and the government, debts to suppliers, and debts to the business owner.

THREE CATEGORIES OF PAYABLES DEBTS

1. DEBT that the company might have to it's employees and to the government

2. DEBT that the company might have to it's customers and suppliers

3. DEBT that the company might have to it's owner(s)

PAYABLES DEBT	LAST MO. ENDING DEBT	TOLERANCE (BUDGET)	Reduction TARGET (X.95)	Reduction ACTUAL
ACCRUED PAYROLL Unpaid	$	$	$	$
ACCRUED BENEFITS (Y-T-D)	$			$
UNPAID TAXES (all)	$		$	$
COMMISSION ACCNTS	$	$	$	$
NON-CANCELABLE POs (w. penalties, interest)	$	$	$	$
CUSTOMER PRE-PAYMENTS (up to 89 days) for contracts	$	$		
SUPPLIERS - TRADE PAYABLES	$	$	$	$
UNPAID OVERHEAD ITEMS	$	$	$	$
SHADOW PAYABLES (informal loans to OWNERS)	$	$	$	$
LOANS PAYABLE TO OWNERS	$	$	$	$
CURRENT LOANS (1-12 mo. NON-OWNERS (Banks, Cards)	$	$	$	$
TERM LOANS (13 mo. +) NON-OWNERS (Banks, Cards)	$	$	$	$
TOTALS:	$	$	$	$

(Table overlay labels: EMPLOYEES & TAXES; CUSTOMERS, SUPPLIERS & OVERHEAD; OWNERS)

"**Critical** debt is the debt that should be your highest priority. That's any debt to employees and to the government. These are Gitmo's favorite debts, because if left unattended for even a short time, they can bring you to your knees and close you down.

"**Necessary** debts are the payables to trade suppliers who keep your company in motion. Gitmo fancies these debts because they are tough to deal with and they often interrupt you and prevent you from growing.

"**Helpful** debt is the debt payable to you as the business owner."

"Helpful? What in the world is a helpful debt?" I begged to know.

"Helpful debts are debts that make you better off when you actually owe people. You might be better off loaning your own money to your company at a higher interest rate than your company might pay going to an outside bank. Your loans are still company debts. They are now debts owed to you, with income to you."

"You got me there. So how does this work?" My question needled him.

"Here ya go. Suppose you want to grow your business. Maybe you need a new gadget. Maybe you want to hire a new employee but they won't be productive for a few months. Perhaps it's time to upgrade your website. Whatever it is, when you plan it all out you calculate that, after you buy and install your new gadget, you will earn 25% more money every year than your principal loan payments cost you. This 25% is your return on your investment, yes?"

"Yes, I'm good so far."

"But you don't want to chew up all of your personal or business savings to buy the gadget. So you borrow the total gadget cost from a bank, and now the bank loan is a debt of the company."

"Keep going."

"Let's say that the cost of the money you borrow, the interest you will pay to the bank, is 8% of the total loan amount. So your payments, principal plus interest, are now 33%. But every year you will keep getting your ongoing net profit of 25% for putting your gadget to work, over and over. Eventually, after your gadget and your 8% interest is paid, you keep earning the 25% profit on your investment."

"I've got it. I'm familiar with ROI. I know how that all works. Anything else?"

"What if you personally borrowed the money from some bank with the interest of 8% and loaned the total money you borrowed to your own company at 1.5% per month balance, which is 18% per year?"

"Ok, so I make my 25% profit from the gadget, plus another 18% interest on my own money, or 43% profit. I pay the bank its 8% and I keep 35%, which is 10% more than my originally planned 25%?"

"Yes."

"C'mon, Mr. Kanketa. That's a bunch of silly games I wouldn't have time for. Are you playing games with the money? Why don't you just say that I am making a 35% profit, which is my 25% ongoing return on my investment, plus 18% more that I charged my company in interest, after the 8% cost of my loan has already been deducted. It's simply a 35% return on my investment."

"Because the 18% plus the 8% interest is a 26% tax deduction to your business before you have your 25% profit. Yes, you will personally earn the added percent on your money that is income to you, but now you have control of the interest income and the taxes that you will owe on it. Now let's add it up."

Mr. Kanketa walked to a whiteboard on a side wall of the gym and began to draw out the plan with a dry marker. I watched intently.

"Right now, today you're probably already earning 3% on your personal money in some savings account."

"Good guess."

"This 3% is income to you. So, why would you use your own money and deplete your savings to buy the gadget?"

"Good point."

"Instead, you borrow the money from a bank at whatever they charge. Let's use 8%, which is 5% higher than using your own money. So, instead of losing the difference, you will personally borrow the money and loan it to your business at a higher interest of 18% more than the bank is charging you."

"And you came up with 18%, how?"

"It's fair and reasonable that you charge what credit card companies charge. That's why we're using 1.5% per month times 12 months."

49

"Fair enough."

"Now, add your 18% interest earned from your investment to the 3% from your savings or investment account, and you are now earning 21% a year on your money before any net profit on the gadget itself. Stock markets rarely promise that kind of return. I would call that helpful, wouldn't you? This is how all the big boys play."

After I added it all up, it dawned on me that there is some pretty good money in the interest game. "That's a great idea, but it doesn't sound legal."

Mr. K. lambasted my ignorance. "The tax laws are set up so you can avoid, but not evade, taxes. Evading is hiding, and that is against the law. Avoiding is legally taking advantage of the laws that are in place. This is lawfully avoiding taxes."

"Great. I'll just turn it all over to my accountant."

"A big word of caution. Would you ever hire someone to eat dinner for you?"

"Not quite," I laughed aloud. "Even if it were possible, they'd probably eat all the wrong things, and I'd be dead in twenty minutes. I'd have to be very specific about their diet."

"Precisely. Eating is critical to your health. There are certain business practices that are critical to your company's health. But you must learn and follow all of the basic survival rules yourself. Don't count on anyone else, not even your accountant, to do your tax dieting for you. They won't always know your intention about every dollar you spend. They'll have to do some guesswork, just like you will. They will never know your business like you will, and inevitably, they will misapply some expenses to the wrong accounts. Correct for government compliance purposes perhaps, usually to the tactical advantage of avoiding taxes, but not always to your best strategic advantage in running your business. I'm not against accountants by any means. But most good accountants will agree, you'll save taxes in the current year, but if they don't know your big-picture strategy—which can only come from you—you could lose big-time in the long-term.

"Your accountant's job is to be sure the government correctly receives the information you provide. Identify and label your expenses yourself. It's easy, and it's a great habit to develop. Don't rely on your accountant to do this. Sure, there's a little training you will need, and there's some paperwork involved for doing it yourself. You have to make up a legal loan agreement from yourself to your business. You will put the interest you will charge your company into the agreement. But creating loan agreements is not your accountant's job, and they might not do this for you. Stay in the ring and learn from your own moves."

"I thought I was trying to lower the company's debt. Aren't I just creating more debt by charging myself higher interest?"

"Debts paid to you as the business owner for loans that you give to your company at an interest rate that is higher than you can earn on your investment anywhere else is helpful to you in the long run. Yes, they are still debts. But the secret is to control your debt picture, not eliminate it. You want to have 2, 3, and even 4 income dollars to every debt dollar."

I was starting to catch on. "So if I'm understanding you correctly, the goal is not to try to be debt-free. The goal is to maintain a consistent profit while containing and managing all debts, right?"

He grinned at me in acknowledgement before he spoke.

"Gitmo assumes you know nothing about this and hopes you push the paperwork aside until it's too late. He hopes you will have 2,

3, and 4 dollars of debt to every dollar of income. If you want to win this round, here's my advice. Always focus on the match, not the round. Stay aware. Is Gitmo making short-term progress, but wearing you down overall? Are you conserving your strength from round to round or are you using it all up too early? Experienced boxers call this 'pulsing.' Pulsing is only doing what you absolutely must do to keep up with the competitor to wear him down. Nothing extra. Nothing more. Nothing less."

Just then, the light went on for me. I was beginning to worry about and react to every little debt instead of keeping my eye on the big D-T-I picture.

"Balance, my friend, balance. Debt isn't all bad. In fact, debt can be very good, if you manage it and keep it in its corner. It's just that Gitmo Debt is a dirty fighter and doesn't play fair. Rather than worry constantly about your debt payables, it is a much more worthy idea to monitor and manage the overall balance of all of your debts."

Kanketa broke the conversation with a sneeze, but politely covered his mouth with a handkerchief, demonstrating manners and refinement.

"Balance prevents unforeseen surprises from often overlooked and underestimated debts. They might not be a problem at the moment, but they will unexpectedly punch your lights out when you aren't looking."

"Mr. Kanketa, as long as I am paying you for this coaching, I will need to understand how business scoring works before I get into the ring. Will you please stop here and take some time to explain these definitions? I am not familiar with some of them."

"Yes," he said. "It's the very first training everyone needs before they have a business." He had anticipated my request, and was quite prepared with eloquent answers.

"There are twelve debts that impact your business scoreboard. Three categories of debt with four kinds of debt in each. The categories are debts to your employees and the government, debts to your customers and suppliers, and debts to you as the owner of your business. These are displayed in the order of importance. Your employees and the government can shut your business down on a dime. Your customers and suppliers can close you down over time.

"And you will close your own business down if you aren't getting your own loans repaid. And here's the biggie. Every decision you make, every action you take, every single swing will affect the D-T-I scoreboard—a point gained, or a point lost. By all means, you must know their definitions by heart."

This was the training I was waiting for.

"You can be absolutely sure of one thing," Kanketa promised. "Gitmo Debt and his cronies know these debts upside and down, backwards and forwards. You just have to know them better."

Session 5: Debts To Employees And The Government

PAYABLES DEBT	LAST MO. ENDING DEBT	TOLERANCE (BUDGET)	Reduction TARGET (X.95)	Reduction ACTUAL
ACCRUED PAYROLL Unpaid	$	$	$	$
ACCRUED BENEFITS (Y-T-D)	$			$
UNPAID TAXES (all)	$	EMPLOYEES & TAXES	$	$
COMMISSION ACCNTS	$	$	$	$
NON-CANCELABLE POs (w. penalties, interest)	$	$	$	$
CUSTOMER PRE-PAYMENTS (up to 89 days) for contracts	$	$		
SUPPLIERS - TRADE PAYABLES	$	CUSTOMERS, SUPPLIERS & OVERHEAD	$	$
UNPAID OVERHEAD ITEMS	$	$	$	$
SHADOW PAYABLES (informal loans to OWNERS)	$	$	$	$
LOANS PAYABLE TO OWNERS	$	$	$	$
CURRENT LOANS (1-12 mo.) NON-OWNERS (Banks, Cards)	$	$ OWNERS $	$	$
TERM LOANS (13 mo. +) NON-OWNERS (Banks, Cards)	$	$	$	$
TOTALS:	$	$	$	$

DEBT #1 of 12:

Unpaid Payroll

"The first four debts are non-negotiable and can cause the biggest problem."

Patiently, I stood there as he proceeded to explain.

"The first debt happens when employees hold payroll checks. This debt is the total amount of undeposited and uncashed checks that are considered unpaid payroll," he explained. "Left unattended, it will cost your business an arm and a leg."

I nodded agreeably. "I can see how an uncashed employee paycheck is definitely a business debt." I thought I was adding levity when I added, "Yeah, ha! And while we're at it, what about my paycheck?"

Mr. Kanketa didn't find as much humor in my remark as I did. "What about it?" he asked. "If you are an employee in your company, what makes you different? Like everyone else, if you are holding your paycheck, it's a company debt until you cash it."

He brushed over my question lightly, but I took his words to heart.

DEBT #2 of 12:
Unpaid Benefits

We were already thirty minutes into our fifth training session and already halfway through Kanketa's program. I was still working up a good sweat with the dumbbells as Mr. Kanketa paraded through the attributes of each debt.

"Unpaid benefits are any accrued vacations that you might have agreed to with your employees but are still unredeemed. Don't overlook reimbursement for health expenses, promises made for gym memberships, car and gas allowances, overtime, and just about anything that you call an employee benefit," he added. "The state is almost always on the side of the employee, so the best policy is to specify your benefits clearly and in writing."

He motioned me to stop the dumbbell extensions and catch my breath. "I think you are now ready for the punching bag." He gave me a nudge and positioned me firmly in front of the lighter of the three inflated punching bags that hung from the ceiling.

"Give it a hit, and remember what we said about never hitting the bag as it is coming toward you. Always hit it as it is swinging away from you."

I began to hit the bag slowly until soon I felt the continuous rhythm and motion of the bag as it returned.

"Hit . . . 2. Hit . . . 4. Hit . . . 2. Hit . . . 4. Hit . . . 2. Hit . . . 4. That's the rhythm of the punch."

"I feel it, Mr. K., I feel it."

"Keep it going. Hit . . . 2. Hit . . . 4. Hit . . . 2. Hit . . . 4. That's also the monthly rhythm of your business. Think monthly," he ranted. "Monthly!"

We punched the bag for twenty minutes straight. I was sapped of energy.

DEBT #3 of 12:
Unpaid Taxes

"Now, I want to get you in top condition for your taxes. Gitmo is going to try to clobber you silly here because he knows that tax-paying is critical to your operation. It's a real weak link for most small businesses. His strategy is that you miss some tax payments, and that will stop you in your tracks from being able to get a loan. No one gets a loan from anyone if they have unsettled tax debts. Even though a loan is a debt, he doesn't want you to get a loan to grow your company. A growth investment produces a profit and a profit pays off debts That would wreak havoc on old Gitmo. This will cause your D-T-I score to improve steadily and that will really throw him into a tizzy."

"That's what I'm here to do!" I howled over the loud beat of the bag. By this time, the volume of his voice had also escalated to match mine. Soon, we were both yelling.

"If you have employees or payroll, you are required to pay Social Security and Medicare, and pay state sales and use tax! These are non-negotiable, and come with high interest and penalties. They are always your highest priority!"

Yes, Mr. Kanketa . . . a priority!" I was breathing heavily and had to grab at my words, throwing them back at him to keep up the continuity.

DEBT #4 of 12:

Unpaid Commissions

The training was moving along steadily, and the evening was quickly coming to a close. I kept trying to hear Mr. Kanketa over my slams of the punching bag. I found myself clinging to every word. I felt my confidence building with every punch.

"Verbal agreements to pay finder's fees and commissions count as debt. Never use the term 'kickback.' Even worse, never make casual promises to give someone stock or a 'piece of the action.' The most innocent remarks often hold up in court under oath. Always be prepared to back up your most offhand comments in writing. The best practice is, don't do it.

"These types of promises are legitimate, court-recognized debts. Make all promises for compensation formal. Put them in writing."

"Mr. Kanketa, these are great insights. I have to stop here and absorb what I've learned."

"I agree. We've covered four debts today, and we'll talk through four debts a week for the next two weeks. Twelve in all. The key is to recognize them as they are coming at you."

I left the gym excited. It was a good session.

Session 6: Debts to Customers, Suppliers, Overhead

PAYABLES DEBT	LAST MO. ENDING DEBT	TOLERANCE (BUDGET)	Reduction TARGET (X .95)	Reduction ACTUAL
ACCRUED PAYROLL Unpaid	$	$	$	$
ACCRUED BENEFITS (Y-T-D)	$			$
UNPAID TAXES (all)	$	EMPLOYEES & TAXES	$	$
COMMISSION ACCNTS	$	$	$	$
NON-CANCELABLE POs (w. penalties, interest)	$	$	$	$
CUSTOMER PRE-PAYMENTS (up to 89 days) for contracts	$	$		
SUPPLIERS - TRADE PAYABLES	$	CUSTOMERS, SUPPLIERS & OVERHEAD	$	$
UNPAID OVERHEAD ITEMS	$	$	$	$
SHADOW PAYABLES (informal loans to OWNERS)	$	$	$	$
LOANS PAYABLE TO OWNERS	$	$	$	$
CURRENT LOANS (1-12 mo.) NON-OWNERS (Banks, Cards)	$	$ OWNERS	$	$
TERM LOANS (13 mo. +) NON-OWNERS (Banks, Cards)	$	$	$	$
TOTALS:	$	$	$	$

Five more days clicked by. The end of the next Tuesday's workday brought a light drizzle, but it didn't last long. Traffic wasn't bad, and I made it on time without too much trouble. I wasn't willing to be late. Today was pivotal to my training.

Mr. Kanketa wore a neatly pressed and starched collared red shirt, but the fedora was still his trademark.

"Hey, before we get started, I have to tell ya. I had a strange visit today from two guys by the name of Barry M. Deeply and his assistant Seymour Corts. They said they were electrical inspectors coming to inspect our building. At first I didn't pay much attention. They looked really legit. Had tool belts on and jumpsuits with the logo GD POWER. When I showed them around, they didn't seem as concerned with our power box as they did with our general office condition. Barry Deeply looked around for ten minutes or so, but when I walked into my office I caught Seymour glancing over the papers on my desk. "May I help you?" I asked. He spewed some gibberish, then they left. They didn't touch the electrical box."

Kanketa balked. Wrinkles on his forehead became prominent. As he looked at me, disappointment crawled over his face.

"That, my friend, was Barry M. Deeply."

"Yes, that's what I just said. Barry M. Deeply," I echoed. "I have his card right here. GD Power."

Kanketa grabbed the card and pointed to the GD. "Do you know what that stands for?"

"I presume that's the name of their electrical firm."

"I'm quite familiar with this logo," he wrenched. "This is not GD Electrical anything. Try Gitmo Debt Power. They were frauds. Your company has just been compromised."

I shuddered, then stammered and stuttered, "Y-Y-You mean to tell me that I let spies into my business today?"

"Yes, I'm afraid so," he grimaced. "Barry M. Deeply is Gitmo's trainer. Seymour Corts must have been his assistant."

I was petrified. "Now what?"

"We have to be extra careful from here on. What did you say to them?"

"Barry Deeply asked me if I ever got a shock from an unexpected current. Jokingly, I told him I felt a strong current here and there when I looked over my current payables report. He made some notes. Then, Seymour asked me when was the last time I plugged in my receivables? I told him it's been a while, but I'm planning to do it this week. He looked a little nervous, and took notes. Then the two of them left in quite a hurry. They said they just got a call for an emergency job and would reschedule. I looked out the window for their truck, but they drove away in a car. That's when I became suspicious about their behavior. It was really odd."

Mr. Kanketa winced. "This is not good news!" he exclaimed. "They've seen enough and now know your debt situation. Promise me that you won't talk to those guys again. We don't need any more leakage than we've already got."

"What do you think they were driving at?" I asked.

"They needed a good picture of your payables to create a debt strategy. Exactly what was on your desk?"

"My entire list of payables. Just how bad is it?" I asked in dismay.

"It depends. What do your payables look like?"

"Rather gruesome this month," I reported. "Today was banking day. There were my bank statements for two months with really low balances, two bounced checks, a list of screamers, a receivables aging report, a few undeposited checks from customers, and a payroll report. All in all, they saw almost everything. What do we do?" I pleaded.

Kanketa rolled his eyes. The corners of his mouth turned down in disgust. I could tell that he was completely concerned with the situation.

"All we can do now is train extra-hard. You will have to know everything I know. You will have to double up on your training time. You are in for some real work."

I was apologetic. "I'll do whatever it takes to save my business. Everything and anything."

DEBT #5 of 12:

Unpaid Non-cancelable Purchase Orders

From You To Your Suppliers

"Undelivered, non-cancelable purchase orders from your customers to you are debts that you are obligated to deliver for products and services they have agreed to purchase. Your agreement probably won't be forgiven by the customer without stiff penalties for canceling. Written customer purchase orders to your business belong in this debt bucket. Verbal purchase orders don't count. Neither do incomplete written orders that are missing items, or don't have a specific budget or a defined delivery time."

Debt #6 of 12:

Customer Prepayments, Unearned Income

"Here's something that not many business owners know, and only a fraction observe. It's the law that you may not spend customer money without doing the work. This is called Unearned Income. A prepayment is an unearned income until you do some work against it. You may only spend income after you are able to show some proof of delivery."

I challenged the idea. "Do you mean to tell me that the prepayments have to sit in the bank until after I do the work? I can't afford that. What if I bought supplies and did 20% of the work today and the rest next week?"

Kanketa countered, "Then, today, you can withdraw the cost of the supplies plus 20% of whatever work you can prove you've completed. You have the receipt for the supplies to prove you delivered that work. That's earned income. Suppose you have an hourly charge for your time of $100 for the company and you have completed 20% of a $10,000 job, or the first 20 hours. Send the customer a time-stamped email that gives them a project status update. Job status reports are good enough for courts.

"By maintaining a balanced flow of prepayments to getting work out the door within the current month, your prepayments should give you enough total income, back office and front office income, to always have enough to pay your bills. You only have a problem when you are doing work as fast as prepayments are coming in."

DEBT #7 of 12:
Unpaid Trade Debts

Kanketa jumped from unearned income to another topic that was a bit more familiar to me.

"Costs of suppliers and any people expenses needed to produce your products and services are trade debts."

"Yes, I am fully aware of supplier debts. They come at me every minute of every day nonstop. There's no need to remind me about this one," I rumbled.

"Remember how you agreed to hang your experiences up at the door?" he inserted.

"That I did agree to. Yes."

He pinned me down. "Well then, when will you do that?"

"I thought I did."

"No, you didn't. Not yet. You are still operating on your assumptions and interpretations. You think you know all about supplier debt. Now, hang your experiences up on that hook over there."

He made me walk through the imaginary motion of hanging up my experiences. I felt like a three-year-old.

"Good. Now let's start over. Costs of suppliers and any people expenses needed to produce your products and services are trade debts." He repeated it slowly.

"There are direct suppliers needed to do the work. They are hired from job to job. If you don't have work, they aren't hired. Then there are indirect overhead costs in your business. You always have them. Those suppliers are always being hired whether you have work or not. Those expenses expand and contract with the performance of your business," he explained.

I was quietly listening as I stood there chewing on a delicious slice of humble pie. I realized then that 5% of my business is what I think I know. Another 5% are things I know that I don't know about business. And a full 90% is what I don't know that I don't know.

DEBT #8 of 12:
Unpaid "Non-People" operating and overhead costs

In the interest of keeping the session productive, Mr. Kanketa stepped up his speaking pace. His words were succinct. "Do you understand that your Profit and Loss Statement shows your gross sales minus your cost of goods sold, which are the costs outside your company to do the work?"

"Yes."

"And you understand that what is left is what you call your gross profit, and what I am now calling your margin, yes?"

"Ditto."

"Your margin has three parts. People costs, non-people costs, and a net profit for you, the owner. For now, we will call the non-people costs the everyday costs to operate your business that aren't salaries, like rent, insurance, phone, and so on."

"Got it."

"Now, with all of your experiences hanging up over there on the hook, just for our purposes right here and right now, your manager salaries in your company must equal your non-people costs, which must equal your net profit."

I fidgeted. "You are telling me that I should have three parts to my margin? One-third people, one-third non-people, and one-third net profit?"

"Precisely." He didn't waver. "You have non-people debts to pay every month, don't you?"

I returned emphatically, "A unanimous, overwhelming yes."

"Good, because you will be paying them every single month on time, before they become debts." He was unequivocally stern.

"But, but, I told you that those darn banks won't give me a line of credit! Certainly not what I need. I might not always have the cash available to pay every non-people debt, as you call it."

"Do you trust me? Do you trust what I say?" Kanketa interrupted. "Do you not own a Chevy Malibu? Am I not your Indy race car driver?"

At that point, we were out of session time. Nothing more needed to be said.

I left deep in thought.

Session 7: Debts to Owners

PAYABLES DEBT	LAST MO. ENDING DEBT	TOLERANCE (BUDGET)	Reduction TARGET (X.95)	Reduction ACTUAL
ACCRUED PAYROLL Unpaid	$	$	$	$
ACCRUED BENEFITS (Y-T-D)	$	$		$
UNPAID TAXES (all)	$	EMPLOYEES & TAXES	$	$
COMMISSION ACCNTS	$	$	$	$
NON-CANCELABLE POs (w. penalties, interest)	$	$	$	$
CUSTOMER PRE-PAYMENTS (up to 89 days) for contracts	$	$	CUSTOMERS, SUPPLIERS & OVERHEAD	
SUPPLIERS - TRADE PAYABLES	$	$	$	$
UNPAID OVERHEAD ITEMS	$	$	$	$
SHADOW PAYABLES (informal loans to OWNERS)	$	$	$	$
LOANS PAYABLE TO OWNERS	$	$	$	$
CURRENT LOANS (1-12 mo. NON-OWNERS (Banks, Cards)	$	$ OWNERS	$	$
TERM LOANS (13 mo. +) NON-OWNERS (Banks, Cards)	$	$	$	$
TOTALS:	$	$	$	$

There we were again. The clock was ticking away and at this point, I was feeling very inadequate

"Do you want a protein bar?" Kanketa slammed some change into the vending machine. We stood there and watched the little arm pinch a vanilla and peanut butter protein bar and dump it off the shelf and into the tray below. I thanked him, but respectfully declined. Time was running out, and every precious minute counted. I didn't want anything to break our stride, least of all a protein bar. He proceeded to the next explanation.

DEBT #9 of 12:
Unpaid "Shadow" Payables

I was anxious to hear about whatever was on his mind, but I wasn't about to do this over the loud bouncing of punching bags. We didn't waste any time getting down to the nitty-gritty.

"Knowing Gitmo, I would say that his spies were looking for casual, informal, unwritten loans made to your business by friends and family. These are typically just 'handshake' agreements referred to as 'shadow payables.' You can't recognize them too easily, but they are definitely there, lurking around in the shadows of your company. These are Gitmo specialties, because they are hard to identify and hard to monitor."

"Shadow payables are new to me," I said. "In fact, the whole idea of loans from me to the company is not something that I can say I'm an expert at."

Kanketa validated me. "Don't worry. You're not alone. There are millions of small business owners out there who walk right over this idea every day. They just aren't aware of the power of doing it right, and they never get their real investment back from their company."

DEBT #10 of 12:
Unpaid Loans to Owners

I could see that Mr. Kanketa was thoroughly enjoying his protein bar. He was peeling back the wrapper slowly and his teeth were sculpting the edges of his bites. As I watched him, I wished I would have taken up his offer to buy me one after all. It was probably just nerves grabbing at my taste buds.

"What does 'doing it right' mean? What should I be doing? I need to know. Heck, when we can't afford payroll, I just don't take a salary," I spoke proudly. "After all, I'm the owner. The company bills must come before my own pocketbook."

"Never!" yelled Mr. Kanketa vehemently. Then he proceeded to lay it out with remarkable clarity.

"You are not your business, and your business is not you. You own a business that is separate from you. It's a living, breathing entity recognized by the state. It has income. It has expenses. It has debts. You as the owner also work for this entity, and are paid for your services just like everyone else. If you do work for your company, and your company doesn't pay you, you have loaned your salary to your company."

"But how is this a loan?" I asked.

"In addition to your owner's profit, you are entitled to a reasonable competitive wage when you work in your business, just like any other employee. When you do, you are both an employee of your company and the owner. It's always best to pay yourself the exact same as you would have to pay any employee for the same work. You aren't paying payroll. Your business is. And, because you are not your business, when you don't pay yourself, your company is borrowing your salary."

I looked at him, puzzled. It seemed to make sense.

"So, if I'm hearing you correctly, what you are saying is that every time I don't take my paycheck, I'm actually giving the company a loan?"

"Spot-on," he murmured.

I kept the idea moving. "Then, I must presume that the company should still withhold my taxes just like any employee, regardless of whether I pay myself or not?"

"Right again. That is the company's legal responsibility for every employee."

"And then, I can loan my after-tax salary back to the company at a good interest rate and take it out later tax-free, before the business pays corporate taxes?"

"Absolutely. Any money formally loaned into the company for which you as the owner are looking for a repayment should be included as part of your company's debt."

Mr. Kanketa fired back. "Doing it right is to make your unpaid salaries formal, written, interest-bearing loan agreements. Always. Always. Always. If you don't, this will lose your match faster than any other debt." I'd never seen him more serious. He continued.

"I recommend that you make a note of your salary in your company records and keep this on file. The record I'm talking about is part of your Operating Agreement, which clearly spells out the rules of your company and how it will work. The IRS would look at this closely if you were audited. But if your salary is clearly stated in the Operating Agreement and supported with a loan document, it will be very difficult to disagree with."

"So, what I'm hearing you say is that this is all about unpaid owner salaries that are informally loaned into the company when the owner declines payments for cash flow reasons."

"Correctamundo!" he confirmed.

Just then, I began to feel my growth. "Oh my God, when I think back over all those years that I never did this, the company would owe me a lot of money right now."

"That's why you hired me. Welcome to Training 101."

Debt #11 of 12:
Unpaid Short-term Loans Payable
to Outside Sources to be
Repaid within 12 Months

Kanketa was on a roll. I found it easier to listen to him, and he found it easier to dispense his training secrets.

"The word 'current' means current year. These are short-term loans that are due in 12 months or less to non-owner outside sources such as banks, investment companies, credit card companies, and other lenders. These unpaid loans are usually smaller amounts invested in one-time business reinvestments, the training and setup of new employees that won't be productive for 90 days, or the creation of a new website, and so forth."

Debt #12 of 12:
Unpaid Term Loans
Payable to Non-owner Outside Sources

"Conversely, long-term loans are to be repaid in 13 months or more. The word 'term' means some future time beyond the current year. These are long-term loans that are due in 13 months or more to non-owner outside lending sources such as banks, investment companies, credit card companies, and other lenders. These are typically large amounts invested in roof repairs, large equipment and machinery, or even loans paid back to buy the business."

"Is that it?" I asked.

"That's it for the debt side," he said. "Every move, every decision, every action of you and everyone in your business is going to be based on those twelve debts."

"The dirty dozen?" I was trying to break the ice with a little levity.

"The dirty dozen," he replied. He didn't allow a single space in the conversation for the slightest joke. It wasn't a laughing matter.

CHAPTER 5

INCOME BEYOND THE CHECKBOOK

INCOME	ROW TOTALS	NOTE:
1. CHECKING ACCOUNT DEPOSITS and CASH ON HAND	$	
2. DEPOSITS IN TRANSIT	$	
3. SAVINGS and INVESTMENTS	$	
4. ACCNTS RECEIVABLE 1-30 days	$	
5. ACCNTS RECEIVABLE 31-60 days	$	
6. ACCNTS RECEIVABLE 61-89 days	$	
7. ACCNTS FACTORED, NOT REDEEMED	$	
8. NON CANCELABLE PURCHASE ORDERS (with penalties)	$	
9. UNPAID LOANS owed to Company	$	
10. INTEREST DUE 12 months or less	$	
TOTAL		

"So, if that's debt, what's income?" My questions kept coming faster and faster.

"When you total up all the income and subtract it from the total of all the debts we talked about on Tuesday, all the money left is available to run your business and pay you a profit. I call this your 'Snapshot In Time' because, just like your debts, the income amount will change every day with every punch you throw, every business decision you make.

"Income is a tad more straightforward, but it still has some bends and curves," Kanketa purported. His training was couched in deep resolve.

"Way too many businesses focus on income, income, income. I focus on debt. Certainly, income is vital to growth. But as I said earlier, my philosophy is simple. You might not always win. Just never lose."

Mr. Kanketa was doing a great job fielding my questions so far, but our session was coming to a close. We were just getting started, and I didn't want to go home.

"Let me give you some food for thought. Income is more than just sales. Your total income is all the money you have access to. We'll take this up next time. Don't forget your Indian clubs and your dumbbells. Fifteen minutes each and every morning."

I gratefully thanked Mr. Kanketa and we both left the gym.

That night, I was revitalized. I lay in bed staring at the ceiling. I couldn't sleep a wink. I knew that my contract with Mr. Kanketa was a great move. I knew I would get results if I just remained diligent. I was determined to be fiscally fit.

Session 8: Ten Types of Income

It was Thursday, session eight of ten. Aarrgh! The workday flew by for me and I was ready to hit the gym. Mr. Kanketa was in the workout area waiting for me. I detected his revived enthusiasm about my progress but he was trying not to show it. He wasn't doing a very good job of it.

"Did you eat yet?" he asked.

"Eat? Hell, I haven't had time to check in with Sally. I was supposed to stop off and pick up some odds and ends at the store. Garbage bags and dish soap, to be specific."

"Are you getting into trouble?" he asked.

"No. She knows me too well. The garbage bags can wait. We're good."

"You need some protein. C'mon, dinner's on me. We'll take my car."

Mr. Kanketa never went anywhere without his briefcase. He grabbed the hard rubber handle and yanked it toward him as we made our way to the side door. We walked outside to the curb where his car was parked. It was a vintage '64 silver-blue Pontiac Le Mans with deep-red bucket seats. The red letters on the blue license plate read COLLECTOR. I swooned over the magnificent machine. My heart leapt. Kanketa was a man of mystery. Every visit with him was a completely unique and novel experience.

We only rode two miles to the parking lot of a nearby brightly lit restaurant, Crabby's Crab Shack. It was still early and the area was highly trafficked. He didn't seem too concerned about the car's security.

Inside the restaurant was equally busy. All of the management knew him. It sounded like it was his home away from home.

We were promptly escorted to a wide, rough wooden table with surprisingly comfortable benches. You can easily imagine what tables might look like at a crab shack. Not ten minutes went by before we were ordering . . . you guessed it! Crab legs deluxe. "Gee, Mr. K., this is a pleasant surprise."

"You're entirely welcome," he said without looking up. He flipped his briefcase onto the bench.

Mr. Kanketa didn't waste time. That's what I liked about him. Mr. K. was a get 'r done guy. We launched quickly into the topic of income. There wasn't much small talk that followed.

The conversation was halted for a moment when the warm, tasty, all-you-can-eat crab legs arrived. It was a great choice for a weeknight. Thankfully, we were sitting in a corner and we could hear each other easily.

His income definitions were refreshingly short and simple. They required less explanation than the debts. Nonetheless, he didn't miss a trick.

"Here's where income makes all the difference. You've got to pay for meals like this from somewhere." We resumed the discussion.

I wondered why Kanketa had his briefcase with him at dinner. The answer soon became apparent. He was a visual kinda guy.

We found enough space at the end of the long wood table to spread out his visual aids. The income sheet was very different than I imagined.

INCOME	ROW TOTALS	NOTE:
1. CHECKING ACCOUNT DEPOSITS and CASH ON HAND	$	
2. DEPOSITS IN TRANSIT	$	
3. SAVINGS and INVESTMENTS	$	
4. ACCNTS RECEIVABLE 1-30 days	$	
5. ACCNTS RECEIVABLE 31-60 days	$	
6. ACCNTS RECEIVABLE 61-89 days	$	
7. ACCNTS FACTORED, NOT REDEEMED	$	
8. NON CANCELABLE PURCHASE ORDERS (with penalties)	$	
9. UNPAID LOANS owed to Company	$	
10. INTEREST DUE 12 months or less	$	
TOTAL		

Income #1.

Checking Account Deposits and Cash On Hand

"What's this?"

"It's your income."

"Income? Are you kidding me? I see ten items here. Ten!"

"Thank God that's all," Kanketa replied. "Income is more than just sales. Whenever you don't account for all of your income, it falls through the cracks of your business and is lost forever."

"Ok. This I really need to hear," I replied.

"Your total income is all money that you have access to, sitting in every crack and crevice at the moment. Some of it is in obvious places, like bank accounts. Other money is not so obvious, but nonetheless, it's still there and it still counts. The objective is to total up all of the money in your checking accounts, all the cash you have on hand, all the checks in the mail, the money in your savings and investments, your accounts receivable that everyone owes you, contracts, loans that you gave to others who haven't paid you back, interest, everything!

"Rule number one. Count all checking account balances, all cash drawers of undeposited money, all credit card deposits. Count everything that is in the bank right now, at this very moment. Your bank account is your snapshot in time. Your banker buddies look hard at your average daily bank balance. After all, they make money with larger balances, not small ones."

"I see. And what about credit cards?"

"Throw all of your credit card sales into this category as well. The deposit wait time is too short to bother with," he indicated. "Also include any petty cash you have in a lock box at the office."

The crab legs were getting in the way. Between the sounds of snapping, cracking, and popping of the shells in the steel grips, he continued.

Income #2.
Deposits In Transit

"The check's in the mail when you have some evidence that your payment is in process. You might have gotten this verbally or in some email verification. The bottom line is that you can verify the check number. This is deposit in transit income."

In between bites of food, I was furiously taking notes.

Income #3.
Savings and Investments

"You can't count any money in savings that you have already pledged for another loan. Only free and clear money that is sitting in your savings or investment accounts at the moment that is not pledged or attached to some loan goes into income category number three.

Income #4.
Accounts Receivable 1–30 days

"Regardless of what plans you have for your Accounts Receivable for the month, they are for all work already completed within the current 30-day period."

Income #5.
Accounts Receivable 31–60 days

"Next, we go to the money owed to your business from customers who have not yet paid after 30 days, but generally pay in less than 60 days. We will separate these receivables, since they are coming from customers who are using you as their bank. This money generally has, or should have, a built-in interest charge to these customers attached to your bill. When the bill and interest are paid, the interest will have to be logged separately upon receipt as income."

"This Accounts Receivable money is considered to be factorable. You will want to look closely at factoring. Factoring is ideal when your bank is not being terribly cooperative with giving you a line of credit."

"Factoring? I've never heard of factoring."

"This is why I asked you to hang your experiences up at the door. Most small business owners don't know that you can sell these receivables to a factoring company and get your money now. The factoring company collects the money from your client at a fair interest rate equal to bank interest."

Income #6.

Accounts Receivable 61–89 days

"Money owed to your business beyond sixty days is approaching the risk point. At the eighty-ninth day, banks and factoring companies will no longer lend money using the receivable as collateral. You may still sue your customer for the money, but the banks consider receivables older than 89 days to be bad debts."

Income #7.

Accounts Factored, Not Redeemed

"If you decide to factor, the factoring company makes a promise to purchase your receivables, but has not given you the money yet. This is generally a small window of time, usually within five business days from the time you submit the receivables for the payment that you are waiting for. But if you use factoring routinely, you will usually have unredeemed money in transit. This money in transit is in its own income category."

Income #8.

Non-Cancelable Purchase Orders From Customers

"It is acceptable to count non-cancelable purchase orders from your customers as income before the work is delivered. A Non-cancelable Purchase Order is always written, and typically carries significant penalties and interest if canceling is necessary."

We took a short break in the conversation.

"The legs were superb, outstanding. Would you like some dessert?" he invited.

"The crab legs took care of me pretty well. I think I'll pass on dessert. Thanks anyway. I'm in training."

I wanted to get the rest of the income picture. I knew that if I didn't finish the discussion, I would lose continuity. I requested that we finish up over a coffee. He agreed.

Income #9.

Unpaid Loans Owed To The Company

"Some companies help fund the key suppliers they rely on. Unpaid loans in this income bucket are principle amounts only. Interest earned from these loans falls into a separate interest income bucket."

Income #10.

Interest Owed To The Company

"All interest income is reported in a separate category for tax purposes. Interest and penalties for late payments from customers are usually charged to the customer at 3%. It is a good practice to divide your final quotes price by .97 as a standard practice to get the new customer price for your products and services. Then, offer a 2% discount to all customers for early payment. The extra 1% covers the smarty-pants customers who are bullying you just because they can. They take the discount and are still late.

"If you give loans to suppliers, employees, and other individuals, 1.5% is a good average interest rate to charge every month on the unpaid balance. That's the highest interest you should charge that keeps you in line with credit cards."

D-T-I Is The Single-Most Important Number In Your Business

"So . . . there you have it. The dirty dozen debts and the ten income items. Everything you need to calculate your D-T-I. And just remember this: Regardless of anything, the size, the type, the location, your product or service offer, your length in business or any other way to assess, describe, or think about your manufacturing business, your service business, and even your non-profit, beyond your net profit, your D-T-I will tell you how healthy and valuable your business is at any moment, regardless of what your accountant's financial statement shows. And if you are running your business correctly and in balance, this number will ultimately reflect the true profit that is in your checking account.

"All businesses on the planet have a D-T-I score at every moment of their existence. D-T-I exactly defines the condition of a company at any specific point in time.

"Now, I'm going to hardwire you to a rule about your income. You might be able to fool the referee. But you can't fool yourself." His off-sided comment came from out of nowhere.

"Never, never, never hide one dime because you think that somehow the IRS won't find it and you won't pay taxes on it. It's true they might not. But that is not the goal, and is dangerously bad business. When people buy or lease your company, they will want to see every penny of income, because it is income that makes your company valuable to your buyers.

"The more income you show, the more valuable your company is. Always deposit every penny. Show every penny. Hiding income gets you nowhere."

We finished up and he paid the bill. The waiter seemed quite delighted to see what was on the receipt. I suspect that Mr. Kanketa was as generous with his tip as he was with his information.

The short ride back to the gym was the same pleasurable ride. He dropped me off next to my car. However, I can say with a high level of surety that if I ever beat Gitmo, there will definitely be a classic Le Mans in my future.

CHAPTER 6

THE BUSINESS LIFE CYCLE

Session 9: Eight D-T-I Positions

Seedling	Critical	Organic Growth	Transition
Startup	Necessary	Acquisition	Exit

BUSINESS LIFECYCLE

STARTUP   RECOVERY   GROWTH   EXIT

Hootie And The Blowfish Couldn't Have Done It Better

Remember Hootie and the Blowfish? They rocked out. I would see them every chance I got.

Right now, that is one group on my list that is going to have to wait. They are in concert tonight and here I am, trading them for boxing lessons. I'm somewhat bummed about that. In fact, I'm getting angrier about this debt thing by the minute, and in some ways, it's probably good that I am. It's helping my resolve.

Here I am once again, at a musty, old boxing gym when I could be in the audience of a thousand screaming beer drinkers. "Gitmo," I mumbled to myself under my breath. "I vow to make this all worth it. I swear I will."

I zipped into my shorts and gym shoes. As I walked out of the locker room, there was Mr. Fedora himself. Mr. Kanketa was carrying a long, thin tube. Probably another one of his training techniques. I didn't stop to question it. Still trying to shake off my anger, I finally had to corner Mr. K. The need for a bigger picture was starting to prey on my mind.

"Mr. K., we've come a long way and indeed I'm grateful. But where is this all going? I'm training my ass off for this one match. Even if I was lucky enough to win against Gitmo Debt, he'll be coming back for more . . . forever. He isn't just going to lay down and admit loss. He won't retire from fighting. It's who he is. If it isn't this match, it will be the next match, and the next, and the next."

A smile covered his face ear to ear. It was the first genuine smile since I told him about GD Power.

"Finally, you understand the meaning of owning a business. Your fights will be in place for as long as you own your company."

I grimaced. "Tell me no," I implored. "I can't do this for the next decade. It's not in me!"

"Every business that exists on the planet today, or has ever existed, either fails, closes prematurely, or will pass through eight rounds or four stages of performance conditions . . . even if for a microsecond. From the minute you are assigned your EIN number to the minute you no longer own the company, your business will have naturally moved through all phases of your business life cycle: the startup phase, the recovery phase, the growth phase, and the exit. This is the path you are on by default. From your original germ of an idea to recovery, growth, and exit, round by round, your company will always be in the ring until it no longer exists.

"Big companies use D-T-I routinely as a tool for decision-making. Unfortunately, D-T-I, debt to income, is rarely used as a management tool in small businesses, and the owners do not get the benefit of knowing at any moment whether their company is healthy, safe, and beating the odds, or tumbling to the mat headfirst.

"When you aren't feeling great, what is the first thing you might do? I'm hoping that you will say, take my temperature. And when you suspect your business is sick, what can you do going forward? I hope that you will say, take the temperature of the business. The goal is to take your company's temperature every single month, just after the last payroll. D-T-I is how you want to formally close out your month."

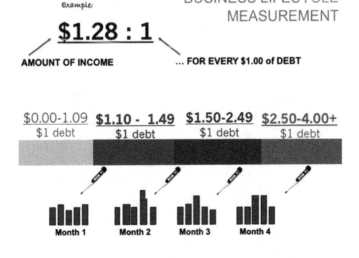

My next question was appropriate. "How do I get enough stamina to permanently keep up with Gitmo?"

His answer came without a thought. "Punch to the right. Always to the right."

The Business Referee: 40 D-T-I Markers

"This, my friend, is your boxing ring, the milieu of your business, with its ropes, its mat, its corners and center ring. Here is where you will meet Debt head-on. Match by match, fight by fight. You will be in and out of these D-T-I positions for as long as you own your company."

"There are eight different performance positions, or company conditions, that your D-T-I score will reveal. Look at them as your business referee."

8 DTI POSITIONS		ORGANIC GROWTH	Grow from within with existing resources
"SEEDLING"	A Concept! No significant income. A Hobby. Gross Sales of less than $50k/year		
		GROWTH BY ACQUISITION	Consider buying another company or business assets to expand
STARTUP	Small income. Monthly gross profit between $3k and $10k		
CRITICAL RECOVERY	Cash poor. Could slip into bankruptcy	TRANSITION	Ready to Exit. Successor is not identified.
		EXIT	Implementing an Exit plan.

"The eight positions are defined by D-T-I markers that a business owner should be concerned with. There are D-T-I scores to match each position. The scores begin at the Seedling position of less than $1.00 to $1.00, which is bankruptcy. The scores end at the owner's profitable exit from the business at $4.00 to $1.00 or better."

How well your business is performing is not subjective. You do not have the privilege to determine the success of your business. There is no guesswork or personal idea of how well you are doing. Your D-T-I is a hard number that dictates your company's strength and value."

"So. It's really not the profit of the business, like everyone seems to think, but the D-T-I marker?"

Kanketa's eyes lit up like a Christmas tree.

"Make no mistake. Your profit is nonetheless your critical business fuel that needs constant replenishment. Your business practices and tools act as the electrolytes of your business that help you retain the profit lost that you sweat out as you pay your bills. It is always your D-T-I score that tells you whether you are winning or losing profit."

"So you're telling me that each of the eight conditions are dictated by my D-T-I score and they are not my attitude about my business or my intention for it?"

"Right on," Mr. Kanketa pointed out. "The Seedling is only a label for a company in the process of formation. The owner has a concept, a germ of an idea about the business. The Seedling could be producing $49,000 a year and the owner could be perfectly happy with that income. But, by D-T-I standards, a Seedling is still not more than a hobby if the total sales are less than $50,000 a year, which is a little more than $4,000 a month. At this amount of annual revenue, the Seedling could be paying all of its obvious debts on a timely basis, but at this level of income, the D-T-I will show many hidden debts that the owner is not considering."

"I see. Take me through this. I'm not quite sure I understand the different levels."

Mr. Kanketa launched into his teaching mode. It was clearly where he was most comfortable.

"A Startup is a new company—in business less than one year. After paying all costs to produce its products and services, the Startup has between $3,000 and $10,000 a month left to pay its salaries and overhead after its production costs.

"A Startup leaves the nest to enter the Critical Recovery phase, often being short of cash. Critical Recovery is the most risky part of the match. Critical Recovery is the highway to the danger zone. There's no bank support for growth. One wrong move and it's lights out for the business. If the business survives Critical Recovery, the banks will take notice and start to buy you tickets for games and

Starbucks coffee cards. This is where they begin to take interest in your account."

"I presume you are talking about Necessary Recovery on your chart?"

"Good job, Hawkeye. Necessary Recovery is a point for maintenance, not aggressive growth. There are operational corrections that must be in place before any attempts at growth should be made. If you try to grow quickly in this phase, before you install or repair your immature business systems, you will chew up your profit too quickly and you'll run out of money. The ironic thing is that the banks will now loan you a little money, but rarely, if ever, loan you what you need. Then, they have your company and your assets tied up and they are in the driver's seat of all growth decisions for your business until the loan is completely paid off. Necessary Recovery is the next danger point because not treated properly, it could keep your company in limbo for years."

Mr. Kanketa took a moment to stretch before resuming. As he was talking, I felt sheepish. This is exactly where I was at the moment.

"What about an investor?"

"Are you serious? Never consider an investor in an early D-T-I range. That's the wimpy way out. Master your business first. There are plenty of programs to give you business development money. Of course, it all depends upon how hard you want to train and how much profit you want to keep in the long run. With an investor who owns more than 20% of your stock, you lose more control than you think. Their investments are protected by something called minority shareholder rights. They can tie you up in court for years. Share profits, but don't give away the store. I recommend against early investors at all costs. Investors know little or nothing about your business and you will trade your hopes and dreams for today's short-term comfort cash.

"If you must, then at least wait until you are in a much higher D-T-I position. My personal opinion, of course."

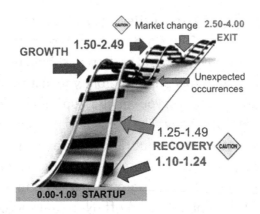

"Continue," I beckoned.

"From organic growth, to growth by acquisition, and finally to the owner's transition and exit, the company is well on its way to its destination. Every business will touch 40 mile markers at some point along the way. Some stops will be short. At other times, the interruption could be very long-lasting, sometimes for many years. The length of the stops are determined by the passion, drive, priorities, and comfort of the business owner.

"Remember, it's your D-T-I trend, not your score, that counts. You'll never have complete control over your D-T-I score. Life happens. Your D-T-I will be constantly barraged by social, technological, economic, environmental, political, ethical, and demographic changes of age, education, and income."

Perception or Reality?

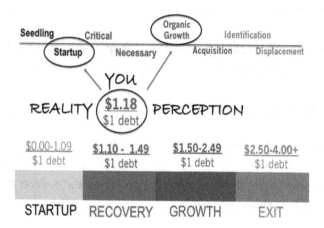

"Here's another little cautionary tale that will shape your success story. Are you operating with perception or reality?"

"How would I know this?" I asked.

"When someone asks you, how's business? and you reply, Oh, my God. Never better! We can't fill orders quick enough. Profits are going through the roof, stop and check yourself. This is the language of a lot of bankrupt companies about 60 days before they file, unannounced to everyone, including their suppliers."

"I'm not going to stop and take everyone's D-T-I after asking how their business is doing."

"No. But you can be on the lookout for some signs of low or sinking D-T-I. Stay aware. Keep your guard up and your ears open. Even from employees of your best customers, you might hear things like:

"Our business is having difficulty getting financing;

"Good people are leaving us. Employee morale is poor;

"Bankers and suppliers are scrutinizing our business closely;

"We just lost a major customer;

"Sales have been declining over the last 90 days, or have been flat when significant growth is expected;

"Our competitors are taking business away;

"We have unpaid tax bills;

"We have outstanding payables beyond 30 days. We don't pay suppliers in less than 45 days;

"We're not meeting payments on a large debt;

"Our debt covenants have been violated;

"Our costs are out of control;

"We are using only a fraction of our capacity;

"We have been experiencing major operating losses;

"Our lenders (and/or suppliers) are giving us a hard time;

"Open up any newspaper, turn to any channel, and you will see businesses going bankrupt. Gitmo just got through with a fight. He beat them, and won big. Take the toy store, for instance. To me it was Tears R Us. I have to admit that I was crushed when their bankruptcy was announced. Toys-Were-Us was my favorite store as a kid.

"Gitmo had a celebration party over that one," he noted. "You might have heard that Toys R Us didn't keep up. Keep up with what? Marketing? Technology? Toy ideas?"

"That's the word on the street," I said.

"Hardly," came Kanketa's discerning remark.

"When Toys R Us filed for bankruptcy, they were making huge profits. Amazon was feverishly delivering their products globally in unbelievable volumes. They had outreach in 17 countries under different brands and licenses. Toys R Us was more than keeping up. And that was the problem. They had the latest apps and covered every aspect of a child-to-young adult imagination. They had food products, party products, baby products, a school product line, you name it.

"They missed only one thing that could have changed the course of their empire. A good D-T-I score. They seemed to have totally ignored their D-T-I ratio. They were clearly focused on their revenue growth and profit trend. Between 1997 and 2015 they went from 784 million in sales to over 11 billion in sales. While their sales continued to increase dramatically, their D-T-I declined steadily since 1997 until they were overextended at the bank."

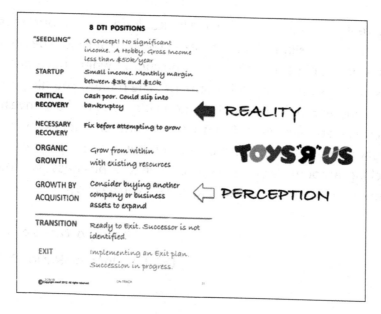

"This translates 11 billion in sales to 5 billion in income to pay for almost 5 billion in debt. Every ounce of the profit was going back out to pay off a debt, with no more money left for growth and no more money left for operating overhead. The Toys R Us little engine that could simply ran out of gas trying to get up the hill. They were spending and trying to grow based on perception, not reality. They defied the basic rules for D-T-I, which took them out.

"The perception? Toys R Us was bringing substantial profits on the sales, even as they were closing their doors. The reality? Toys R Us finally had only .03 cents available to pay for every $1.00 of debt.

"The size of the business doesn't matter. Their D-T-I was overlooked, discovered too late, or reported incorrectly. Most bankrupt companies use every last penny of their often large profits to pay off their debts. And speaking of bankruptcy, here's another little secret. Every business has been bankrupt at one time or another."

I laughed. "Well, not exactly every business, right? There's always Warren Buffet, Bill Gates, Jeff Bezos of Amazon, and . . ."

"Oh really?" I could see that Mr. Kanketa was about to say something revealing. *"Then let me ask you this.* Since the beginning of business tax-paying history, all business owners have been in bankruptcy, even if only for moments. The minute you file papers for a Federal Employee Identification Number, you have invested something somewhere before that EIN number reaches you from the government office. You need the number to open up a corporate checking account. If you have ever owned a business, you have spent more than you have coming in. Yes, you have been bankrupt."

The Importance of your
Debt-To-Income Ratio (D-T-I)

"The total income of your business minus total debt equals the amount of money you have to pay your people costs, your non-people costs, and give you a net profit."

Kanketa gave me a look of antipathy. "Incidentally, some highfalutin banker somewhere in the banking system decided to call it debt to income. Instinctively, you would refer to this as income-to-debt. No . . . it wasn't my idea.

"Most businesses incorrectly state, overlook, or do not divulge at least four of these debt items when calculating their debt, and they continue to inaccurately judge the actual performance and profit of their company."

"It's time to create 12 months of blank income and debt forms like these that you can have on hand at the end of each month. Hold yourself accountable to use these to complete and close out your finances for the month."

INCOME	ROW	TOTALS	NOTE:	PAYABLES DEBT	LAST MO. ENDING DEBT	TOLERANCE (BUDGET)	Reduction TARGET (X.95)	Reduction ACTUAL
				ACCRUED PAYROLL Unpaid	$	$	$	$
1. CHECKING ACCOUNT DEPOSITS and CASH ON HAND	$			ACCRUED BENEFITS (Y-T-D)	$	EMPLOYEES & TAXES		$
2. DEPOSITS IN TRANSIT	$			UNPAID TAXES (all)	$		$	$
3. SAVINGS and INVESTMENTS	$			COMMISSION ACCNTS	$		$	$
4. ACCNTS RECEIVABLE 1-30 days	$			NON-CANCELABLE POs (w. penalties, interest)	$	$	$	$
5. ACCNTS RECEIVABLE 31-60 days	$			CUSTOMER PRE-PAYMENTS (up to 89 days) for contracts	$	CUSTOMERS, SUPPLIERS & OVERHEAD	$	
6. ACCNTS RECEIVABLE 61-89 days	$			SUPPLIERS - TRADE PAYABLES	$		$	$
				UNPAID OVERHEAD ITEMS	$	$	$	$
7. ACCNTS FACTORED, NOT REDEEMED	$			SHADOW PAYABLES (Informal loans to OWNERS)	$	$	$	$
8. NON CANCELABLE PURCHASE ORDERS (with penalties)	$			LOANS PAYABLE TO OWNERS	$	$ OWNERS	$	$
9. UNPAID LOANS owed to Company	$			CURRENT LOANS (1-12 mo.) NON-OWNERS (Banks, Cards)	$	$	$	$
10. INTEREST DUE 12 months or less	$			TERM LOANS (13 mo. +) NON-OWNERS (Banks, Cards)	$	$	$	$
TOTAL				TOTALS:	$	$	$	$

(Printable forms at the back of the book)

"So that's it? That's where this is all going? I'm on a track to the end of my business?" This wasn't a match. This was my first match. I was not terminating Gitmo Debt, just beating him in a match.

"It's your business. Control it, or someone else will."

"Well, now, I guess I have made my decision, heh?"

"It's always yours to make. Learn what you need to know now. I promise you, it will get easier and easier. The better you train now and the more you put into place, the more matches you will win, almost effortlessly."

"Just how many matches are we talking about here?"

"Let's see . . . over the next 48 months, I'd say you are looking at one solid match with Gitmo every ninety days or so. It will take 16 wins to take the title and become a champ for good. Here's the good news: You won't need me around. I'm going to train you well and show you every trick in the book. What you do from there is up to you. No judgements. Just choices and consequences.

"Can I learn it all in these few weeks?"

"Learn it, yes. Master it, no. But mastery is a mind-set. You can master it as soon as you can master it, in 90 days, 120 days, 360 days. You will have all the tools and techniques. D-T-I is the most fundamental to your business. But D-T-I is one of the basic three. There are two others I can train you on along the way."

"What are the others?" I kept diligent in my pursuit of all answers.

"Most businesses aren't set up to make a profit in the first place. They are always in a fight and never know why. Their owners are surrounded with constant stress, mystery, and guesswork. They used to love their business. Now they hate it. It's not an enjoyable experience. The funny thing is that they are bringing in good profit. They just never keep it. It drips right out the bottom of their business like a leaky bucket. They have nothing to show for years of effort and they end up selling their businesses at fire sale prices. I train the House of Value, a perfectly balanced way to keep all the money inside the company. House of Value owners might not always win. They just never lose.

"The third level of the basic three is achieving financial balance. Getting the most profit from your company with the least amount of work and selling or leasing your business for years, even decades, for ongoing income. Achieving financial balance is all about managing income. Financial balance training is all the finance you will ever need for the rest of your career as a business owner and get results."

"I'd really like to get that training, Mr. Kanketa."

"All in good time, my friend. All in good time. Right now, it's Gitmo and D-T-I. This is the language of the day. What do you say?" He glanced at me with nothing less than the highest of expectation.

Mr. Kanketa pumped me up with a renewal of spirit. It was more inspiring than Hootie and the Blowfish. Or even my top ten favorite groups. They would come and go. Kanketa's tutelage would last a lifetime.

Session 10: Those Darn Banks

Session Ten? Already? *You are my sunshine, my only sunshine . . . .* OMG. Time's a wastin'. We're getting down to it. Kanketa's sessions were getting longer as we approached Fight Night.

Dumbbells, twenty minutes. Punching bag, twenty minutes. Learn something new, sixty minutes. A pep talk for the final ten. This is now my new training schedule.

I moved through the first forty minutes routinely. My concentration was high, and not much exchange went on during that time.

He waited patiently as I completed my routine. As usual, he showed up with a briefcase.

As I finished, I barked, "So what do you have for me to learn today, Mr. K.?"

"Remember your casual comment in our first interview? As I recall you said:

That darn bank! They're such small thinkers.

They just can't see the big picture!

I need $50,000. They won't give me fifty bucks!

"Yes, I guess I did," I admitted.

"When was the last time you tried to apply for a business loan and you were turned down?"

"Uhh, just three weeks ago," I remarked.

"Getting bank financing for your business can be very frustrating . . . until you see it from the bank's point of view. Just like you, banks make a profit from selling products and services. Their product for sale is money. Small business banks have a D-T-I sweet spot with their customers between $1.25 and $1.49. This is their ideal negotiating range. This is where small banks can outbid large banks because of their overhead. Above $1.49, all banks are the same and are subject to the same federal compliance and regulations.

"In this recovery range between $1.25 and $1.49, well . . . you're not in critical condition. Your loan is generally a safe bet, and you need some money to take your company to the next level. This is the range in which small banks can latch onto you and grow with you."

Mr. K. opened his briefcase. It was nicely organized, with papers and charts. He pulled out a small picture and laid it on the bench nearby.

"Below a D-T-I score of $1.25, the banks do not make money. Your D-T-I is too small and you're not profitable. It isn't difficult to understand that your account is too small and too expensive for the bank to work with you. But you still need money, and not getting it doesn't help your cause."

INCOME		DEBT
	TO PAY	

Banks will not show

much interest

BELOW 1.25 to 1

Not profitable. Too small.

Kanketa faced me without blinking an eye. "Let me ask you something. Would you ever book a match with a guy like Gitmo without knowing something about him or his record, just because it felt like you could win?"

I boldly returned his question with sarcasm. "Does a monkey have lips? Does Sasquatch sleep in the woods? Certainly I wouldn't consider it. So what's your point?"

"Many small business owners rely on the FEEL of the business instead of the FACTS. The fact might be that the D-T-I score puts them into Critical Recovery and they are technically not bankable, when the owner might FEEL like the company is growing. In general, a bank will loan your business about 40% of the difference between your income and your debt. Suppose your income of the business is $1.20 for every $1.00 of debt. In this case, the bank will loan 40% of twenty cents, or eight cents for every $1.20 of income.

"I should qualify this by adding that if they are willing to give a bigger loan than 40%, they will need to have you pledge your personal assets, such as your house, your car, and other tangible items of value. The problem is that they now own all your stuff and can dictate all future lending. Now that darn bank can decide whether you can grow or not, regardless of the wonderful opportunities that fall in your path along the way."

He fingered through his briefcase for another visual aid.

"When we talk about D-T-I, there is only one goal: keep stepping, keep moving. Step to the right as quickly as possible. The longer you stay in one D-T-I position, the harder it is to move. Every day you will be faced with another business decision that could create debt. And if you forget your place in your life cycle, then what happens? Don't stop. Never stop. Keep moving!"

He pointed his finger and gestured to the right. "How fast you move depends on you. A good rule of thumb is to increase your D-T-I score by ten cents a month.

"One good strategy that has always worked for me is to divide and conquer. By focusing on a small net income increase of .05 cents a month, and a small debt reduction of .05 cents a month, the ten cent overall monthly improvement is much easier to accomplish in a couple of years.

"At first you can go for some major swings and leaps. In fact, you will see your best progress immediately because you hadn't considered the new income and debt types as part of your target. But as you whittle away at the debts, the five-cent target every month will get harder and harder to hit. That's when you should settle down into small deliberate objectives. Five-cent improvements consistently hit every month will do just as much."

(target monthly improvement)

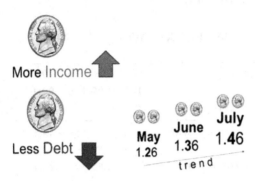

Kanketa's eyes pointed up and left for a moment of reflection. It became evident that he was anxious to share an experience. "If you ever hit the critical recovery point, such as I did in my early years when a major customer that owed my company a lot of money announced bankruptcy without warning . . . We took a huge tumble into Critical Recovery right along with them. Within 60 days, we fell from a D-T-I of $1.68 growth to a $1.22 critical recovery. I didn't see it coming. We did everything possible to recover by improving D-T-I."

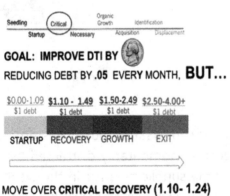

"Tell me, what are you learning? Where do you think you are right now? If you were standing in the ring at this moment, what do you think your D-T-I score would be? How will this knowledge about D-T-I help you in the ring?"

WHERE ARE YOU RIGHT NOW?

"SEEDLING"	DTI	Less than 1.00:1
STARTUP	DTI	1.00:1 to 1:09:1
CRITICAL RECOVERY	DTI	1.10:1 to 1.24:1
NECESSARY RECOVERY	DTI	1.25:1 to 1.49:1
		BANKABILITY
ORGANIC GROWTH	DTI	1.50:1 to 1.99:1
GROWTH BY ACQUISITION	DTI	2.00:1 to 2.49:1
TRANSITION	DTI	2.50:1 to 3.99:1
EXIT	DTI	4.00:1 +

Bill-Paying Is An Opportunity

Bill-Paying Is An Opportunity

I was engaged in the conversation, but his customer story triggered a thought. I became momentarily distracted by a commitment I had made to some suppliers earlier in the week. I sounded off unexpectedly. "Damn. I just remembered. I've gotta pay some bills this week!" Mr. Kanketa seized the moment.

"Bill-paying is rarely anyone's favorite thing to do. Too often, small business owners labor over bill-paying, prioritizing bills emotionally, beginning with the squeakiest wheels. Logic seems to always take a second seat. However, bill-paying is an attitude, and it's all in your perspective. It's a decision opportunity to strengthen your position. You are reducing your debt by paying your bills. This positively impacts the true value and condition of your company. Every swing, every punch at your bills, can make for a higher D-T-I score, and the value of the company goes up another notch."

Does Size of the Business Matter?

"Mr. K., do you think the size of my company matters? Gitmo's so big. Hell, he's twice my size!"

This was one question that Kanketa could handle. He carried legitimate opinions about size. He was smaller in stature than I was. Yet, he'd been victorious in the ring with Gitmo many times. His reply inspired me.

"There are two tenets to overcome size.

"Always stay calm. When you manage to overcome your own mind, your limitations of size become invisible and you rise free above all things. When you are overcome by your mind, you are burdened with concerns and worry. You become subordinate to things, unable to rise above. Mind your mind; guard it resolutely. Since it is your mind that confuses your mind, don't let your mind give in to your mind. Be calm."

"And the second?"

"Be prepared. Preparation reduces fear and then you can concentrate. The size of your business doesn't matter. Neither does your business type. Fully prepared, you can freely concentrate on making a profit, stress-free. You won't get distracted by the detours of constant change that are always going on around you.

"One last word before you go into the ring swinging. D-T-I is a universal measurement for the health of every business; a manufacturer, an insurance agent, a cosmetic specialist, a Bitcoin broker, a doctor, a lawyer, an Indian chief, a bar mitzvah caterer, a school, a non-profit . . . even a church. Yes, a church is a business. Every type. Every size. Including every hobbyist with anything at all for sale.

"Al's Bait Shop could have a high D-T-I score and be able to take out a loan for $200,000, while Toys R Us or Sears, with millions of dollars in profit and a very low D-T-I score, could be turned down. The whole story is about your D-T-I, not your sales, not your profit.

"From the moment you start your business, you're on the business lifecycle track and will have to overcome certain challenges and conditions. You'll have unexpected twists and turns. An unforeseen competitor will blindside you. Social, technological, and economic swings might shake out growth opportunities. Environmental, political, ethical, and demographic changes will catch you by surprise. No matter what moves where, your D-T-I is the only truly reliable number to accurately manage your business with. It always speaks the truth. Low D-T-I scores are the big reason for the high failure rate of Startups. Thousands end up in bankruptcy every year because they didn't pay attention to their D-T-I soon enough, if at all.

"A good D-T-I automatically produces a profit, but not the other way around. A good profit does not necessarily create a good D-T-I. The higher the D-T-I, the more profit ends up in your checkbook. Once you are at D-T-I of $1.50, your net profit should become respectable."

"Mr. Kanketa, I have to know something. Please be ruthlessly candid with me. Do you honestly think I have a chance here? Who do you think will win this match?"

He looked at me, and through me. I'll never forget his next comment. "In any conflict, as in the fight of business, there are two different forces battling each other. Debt is the force of evil, and income is the force of good."

"So, make the goal to be debt-free, and the debts will handle themselves, yes?"

"No, no, no. Never. Remember what we agreed to in our second session?"

Kanketa had the memory of an elephant. I was struggling to keep up with him.

"Debt-free is a myth. There is no such thing as debt-free and the goal isn't to be debt-free. Debt itself isn't bad. It's the uncontrolled, mishandled debt that creates big trouble. Your goal for having debt is to achieve a debt tolerance level.

"Tolerance is the goal. Tolerance is the level of debt that your business budget can comfortably handle. Tolerance is your voice of reason telling you to slow down and pay attention. Your debt is your ability to use and leverage other people's money effectively. It is important to understand that business debt is essential to the health of your business."

"Essential?"

"Let me ask . . . is the goal of your blood pressure zero? Hardly. The goal of your blood pressure is a tolerance of 120 over 80. Is the goal of your body's temperature zero? No. It's 97. Is the goal of your weight zero? The goal of your ideal weight and the health of your body is uniquely dictated by what your body can optimally tolerate."

"I understand. It's about tolerance. But then, why are Gitmo debts bad debts if I can tolerate some of them? Will I win with sheer tolerance?"

"Gitmo's debts are the force of evil. Gitmo debts are debts to tolerance. They go on and on and on. It is a 12-bell tied match. He's pulsing you, doing only what must be done to wear you down. And when you do, you take your eye off the ball and the debts spin out of control. They grow wildly without a plan. He doesn't want you to succeed. Gitmo Debt operates out of fear, impatience, distraction, and ego. Gitmo wants you to look good to others at the risk of taking care of yourself and your family. Gitmo's mission is to make your financial picture so cloudy that you never know where you are, in the ring or in your business. That's the only way that Gitmo stays in control.

"Income is the force of good. You don't always have to win every round, just never lose a match. Income is your measuring stick for your understanding, skills, and for the true value that you bring to your business. Income is the reason behind the reason you got into business. Income makes your life better and allows you to leave your contribution to the world to make a positive difference."

He gave me a coy smile. "Who do I think will win this match? Income or debt? It all depends upon which one you feed."

With tonight's training session ten, I concluded my training for Gitmo. I knew it was only the beginning of what I would need to stay in the game long-term, but Kanketa taught me well. I felt ready, at the height of my confidence. In some odd way, I was anxious to step into the ring.

CHAPTER 7

IT HAPPENED AT FIGHT NIGHT

The slate-gray clouds of the early evening were ominous.

I made arrangements to meet Mr. Kanketa in the locker room an hour before the match. We would go over the rules for scorekeeping.

I snuck in a steel service door in the back of the building, but I did get a glimpse of the line of cars carrying the hordes of curious onlookers. They stretched a mile. One thing was for sure. We can always count on Gitmo Debt to draw a crowd.

Well, there I was. Nervous Nellie. This wasn't just any old fight. This was the fight for my business life. The local tabloids promoted us well.

I thought I had arrived early enough to beat the crazy group of reporters. I didn't. From the locker room, I peered out into the large stadium filling up with enthusiastic fans who were already cheering me on. All of my customers and vendors. My employees. My family and friends. The owners of thousands of ruined businesses. All were there to support me in my fight against my ferocious opponent. I couldn't, and I wouldn't, let them down. Most important of all, I wouldn't let myself down. The stakes were high. I could retire on the prize money. The night was everything I've been training for. That night was my night.

Thanks to Mr. Kanketa, I was well-trained as a fighter and felt confident and prepared. Yet, it didn't protect me from the fight night jitters.

Mr. Kanketa had knocked some reality into me and I was going into this fight with eyes wide open. It was no secret that my D-T-I of $1.05, which made me little more than a Seedling, would need to be dramatically improved. But that night in the ring I planned to change all of it. I knew it wouldn't be easy, but everything I had ever worked for was on the line. I found myself standing up to the biggest bully the business world has ever known, the same guy that took down all my friends' businesses. Thanks to Mr. Kanketa I knew Gitmo's weaknesses, and I planned to use all of them to my full advantage.

Tallying the Score

We had almost an hour before I was called, and I was anxious to hear about D-T-I scoring.

"Now, before you go out there, let me fill you in on how the scoreboard works. I'll monitor it for you now, because it's your first match. But, you will need to learn this sooner rather than later. For tonight, you need to put your full concentration on getting in control of your D-T-I." He spoke in a calm, assuring voice.

"Your D-T-I score is the ticker tape of your personal, private, controllable stock market. It is the Wall Street report of your business. If you excel as a day trader, it promises to pay you better than the DOW ever will. By investing in your debt, you are investing now for permanent, continuous returns later. Some days, your D-T-I will go up a little. Some days, it will go down. But, just like the stock market, it must always climb in an upward trend over time."

That was an interesting perspective, I thought to myself. He was right. My own stock market was a perfect analogy. Then, the idea came to life as he pulled out a chart from his small briefcase.

"Some companies internally post D.T.I. in their lunchrooms and encourage everyone to get involved. Some companies set up rewards and bonuses based on the company's D-T-I score. The D-T-I scoreboard can be customized to display simplicity or degrees of complexity, depending on who in the company is viewing the board for their bonuses. For example, employees in the Production Department of a manufacturing company might only be concerned with the date row and the month-to-month growth in the fourth row."

1/31/2018	2/28/2018	3/31/2018	4/30/2018
JAN	FEB	MAR	APR
		$0.49	$0.59
$0.00	$0.00	$0.63	$1.21
$0.00	$0.00	$0.14	$0.62
$0.00	$0.00	$0.14	$0.62
$3,555.00	$8,753.00	$29,113.07	$29,113.07

(example)

"On the other hand, managers would glue their eyes to an expanded version, since they have a direct impact on each income and debt item."

He dug into his briefcase and unfolded a bigger sheet. His example was well laid out.

"This might give you a better idea," he said.

"The two columns on the far right are your income and debt columns. The column to the left of Monthly Income Actual is an annual income 12-month forecast based on the current month's D-T-I."

QTR	QUARTER END	AS OF MONTH END	DEBT TO INCOME Current Month	FORECAST ANNUAL INCOME	MONTHLY INCOME ACTUAL	TOTAL DEBT Actual
YEAR ONE ACTUALS DTI						
		BEGIN >	.55	$720,000	$60,000	$110,000
1	6/30/2017		.95	$880,850	**$79,845**	**$84,300**
		7/31/2017	.92	$793,224	$66,102	$73,907
		8/31/2017	.89	$793,200	$66,100	$73,900
2	9/30/2017		1.33	$947,860	**$81,050**	**$61,000**
		10/31/2017	1.28	$984,180	$82,015	$64,000
		11/31/2017	1.34	$886,800	$73,900	$55,333
3	12/31/2017		1.64	$924,080	**$80,721**	**$49,356**
		1/31/2018	1.58	$916,800	$73,900	$47,724
		2/28/2018	1.55	$886,800	$73,900	$47,724
4	3/31/2018		1.65	$918,072	**$77,320**	**$46,888**
		4/31/2018	1.74	$927,432	$77,286	$44,445
		5/31/2018	1.73	$898,944	$74,912	$43,181

It was a complex but clean visual. My eyes didn't have to strain to figure it out.

He pointed with exactness. "You can see how the income and debt fluctuate from month to month based on decisions in the company. The date column starts in June. It was the beginning month that Duvall Foods started to track its D-T-I. In the column immediately to the right, you can see how the D-T-I moved each month based on the decisions in the company. It shows the improvements and consequences from managing income and debt payables."

Well, there it was, in living color. My stock market report. I was excited about this and couldn't wait to create my own for our company.

Kanketa dampened my enthusiasm with words of caution. "This might be a good idea for you and your business partners. But your stakeholders and employees might see a simpler, less daunting chart. There are many ways to show D-T-I, depending upon the industry and the involvement of your team. If you only have a few employees who are mostly partners and owners of the business, you might monitor D-T-I monthly, but display it quarterly," he explained.

Out popped another view from his briefcase. Kanketa always came prepared.

"Another way that D-T-I is reported is by showing a monthly forecast tailored to different teams. In this case, the marketing team is more interested and focused on the income side than on debt reduction. Your chart might have a more positive emphasis."

"My advice? Choose transparency, but tailor it to your team. I always preferred this approach. There are many ways to display your company's stock report that is meaningful to your stakeholders. If you are subscribing to D-T-I transparency as a permanent part of your business methods, it will demand constant attention and conditioning. Give your employees enough to draw them in to participate, but not enough to spread your dirty laundry."

I tucked his advice into my mental briefcase as he added a trailer to each thought.

"Every fighter needs a coach/trainer. It is critical to get an outside perspective. But not all trainers are created equal. Like anything else in life, trainers specialize. From boxing to business, you need the right set of eyes to see what you can't see yourself. Running a business might be hard work, but it isn't complicated. Running a business with a specific outcome, within a specific time, is complicated. Nine times more complicated, to be exact.

"Each of the nine equal and inseparable basic functions of a business must move and perform harmoniously. This takes an outside set of eyes and some firsthand experience with each function to know what you are looking for.

"A good business trainer/coach/mentor can make a tremendous difference in your D-T-I improvement. The trainer's responsibility should include design, development, implementation, and management of the entire D-T-I strategy.

"Maintaining accountability and staying on track is the biggest part of the trainer's service. D-T-I is nothing but a mathematical formula. Putting the formula to work in your business is the difference between success and failure. Your D-T-I score can easily slip right through your fingers and you can come up emptyhanded after a lifetime of hard work. This is why D-T-I should be monitored and managed monthly.

"Boxing beginners absolutely need to master the step-drag and pivot maneuvers. This type of movement may seem difficult at first. It's easy for boxing newbies to create a bad habit of lifting their feet during a fight. The veteran boxers will tell you to keep your feet firmly planted on the ground so you're always ready to attack, defend, or move away. Besides, jumping around is a huge waste of energy. The flashy footwork will come naturally once you develop better conditioning and technique.

"If this wasn't true, you would have a $4.00 to $1.00 ratio right now. Find a trainer who understands D-T-I, or is at least willing to learn it. Have your trainer collect your debt and income numbers monthly, and log your D-T-I at the close of each month to track and monitor your true financial improvements. Lean on your trainer to explore options for correcting problems as they happen, before they get out of control.

"Try it for 90 days. If you have the right trainer for the job, you should see dramatic and immediate results in just a few weeks. Why? Because day in and day out you are busy trying to make your business work, and this kind of perspective will be good for you. It just won't always be comfortable. You will want to stay in the game, and you probably won't do this alone. My experience only."

Fight Night Jitters

Just then, through the tinny, sharp megaphone of the D-T-I scorekeepers, my name was being called. We shook hands, and he wished me the luck of the Irish.

As I walked out into the crowd toward the ring, I happened to look over my shoulder. My eye caught sight of Barry M. Deeply, who now had a coach's silver jacket on. It was a step up from the GD Power jumpsuit of earlier days. Seymour Corts was filling the Gatorade cooler.

They both knew that the cat was out of the bag for their little spy trick, but it didn't seem to bother them in the least as they went about their work. There was no appearance of guilt about faking the electrical inspection in my office.

I grabbed the ropes firmly to support my climb into the ring, As I looked up, I saw Gitmo. He stared me down with his typical, over-confident grin. I knew it was his fear strategy. I was ready for him. I managed to maintain my composure as the referee walked to center ring. Then came the all-too-familiar announcement.

"Ladieeees and gentlemen! In this corner we have the world champion of business deeeeestruction. Gitmooooooo Debt!"

The arena was filled with loud boos and hissing as Gitmo moved to ring center and removed his gold plaid fighter's robe to expose his paunch.

The ref barked: "And in this corner is a new Seedling to challenge Mr. Debt's unbeatable deeeeestruction record! Tonight, he hopes to overturn Gitmo Debt's winning streak and take his business back!" My ears popped. I never heard a crowd of fans cheering at such a blistering volume.

"Gentlemen! At the sound of the bell, you will come out fighting!" yelled the referee.

I plugged my mouth with the plastic mouthguard and we squared off with our gloves meeting and returned to our respective stools.

Round 1: THE SEEDLING SERENADE
". . . And There's The Bell!"

ROUND 1

D-T-I   0.01 - 1.00

At the loud clang of the bell, I launched into position and began with footwork in rhythm, as I tried to anticipate Gitmo's every move. My tightly wrapped hands were already perspiring.

I admit that I was a bit shaky. For a few minutes, I was overcome by sheer nervousness. I hoped that the novelty of finally fighting back would soon wear off. The brightly lit D-T-I scoreboard was a pleasant sight. Both Gitmo and I were starting on equal D-T-I terms of $1.00 to 1.

I threw some practice punches into the air. My eyes explored every inch of Gitmo's slovenly, overweight body. "What will be the first punch?" I kept repeating to myself. "From where? In what direction? How hard?"

Then, there it came. His first tactic was to take a swing at my employee debt. Seymour Corts must have found this out from the checks on my desk. When employees have to hold their payroll checks, the total amount of undeposited and uncashed checks are considered unpaid payroll. Unpaid payroll is debt of the company to its employees. For a moment, they had me.

I wasn't terribly surprised. I knew Gitmo loves accrued wages. He is famous for his "unpaid employee" punch. This is his well-known specialty. He brought to the attention of the crowd that someone in my production department was holding a payroll check.

I admit, I didn't have enough money for payroll a few weeks back, and a long-time friend and employee helps me out from time to time by holding his check. Gitmo knew I was still required to pay Social Security and Medicare, state sales and use tax. These taxes are non-negotiable, and come with high interest and penalties.

Luckily, timing was on my side. I couldn't believe I could give the next blow. An unexpected customer check just walked in and caught Gitmo off guard.

He didn't anticipate such a prompt return. I immediately paid my employee with the customer money before anything else. Gitmo was convinced I would buckle and he would pick up points for unpaid payroll debt, which would have happened if I hadn't taken a defensive position.

My next move was to take my D-T-I score, which would now include the incoming customer check as income, and show that I paid off some debt. While this would be an improvement to my D-T-I score, what Mr. K. drilled into me in an early training session just hit me.

Kanketa would always voice that: "Unpaid payroll debt is eliminated on payday. When payroll is disbursed, unpaid payroll should always be zero. All payroll is paid for the moment until it starts to accumulate again in the following week."

I proceeded with caution. If I threw a hard punch and took my D-T-I right now, one week before the upcoming last payroll of the month, I would have to report all payroll that is being accrued for work done in the last week as unpaid. The total payroll would show a bigger debt than the debts that my customer check would pay off.

Pulsing was my strategy. I decided to hold back from taking D-T-I and instead I put my guard up. I kept myself in a holding pattern and avoided D-T-I for the moment. I would never report unpaid payroll for more than one payroll period. Instead, I planned to take D-T-I immediately after the last payroll of the month.

I could see that Gitmo was mad as hell, especially when he saw my D-T-I score inch up eight points. I found myself at 1.08. The crowd went berserk, and a wave of refreshing confidence came over me. In actuality, this punch didn't affect my D-T-I score as much as it could have.

One thing was certain. I knew I wouldn't beat Gitmo if I kept doing what I've always done. He was committed to taking a swing in my weak area again with the unpaid payroll bit. He would keep pounding away unless I made a permanent fix to my system. It was really a sore spot, and I didn't need the constant stress of a repeat performance.

Before my training, I had always paid my employees weekly. I'd since learned that a line of credit would be my failproof strategy. Without hesitation, I had the business apply for a line of credit to cover two months of bills. Then, I changed payday from weekly to bi-monthly. This maneuver stopped Gitmo cold.

It was a dramatically better cash plan to move payroll to the 15th and last day of the month instead of the weekly dribble that constantly drained our checking account, especially when customers didn't pay. By putting my effort into a line of credit rather than expending my energy on the continuous worry over a low balance in the checkbook every Friday, I could ease up on my cash flow and avoid the possibility of late payrolls and unpaid payroll. No one would have to hold paychecks again. It was a solid move.

I watched Gitmo whirl and step back to check his position. Once he realigned his stance, he continued to swing widely and relentlessly with another of his nasty unpaid employee tactics. This time, he returned with a heavy shoulder punch of unredeemed employee benefits.

He started assaulting me with my unpaid health care. Next, he managed to hit me upside the head with my unpaid unredeemed vacation time, and the promises I had made to employees for gym memberships, car allowances, and overtime debts that were still unredeemed. In that moment, I realized where Gitmo got his information. Seymour Corts, the GD Power spy, must have seen my benefits report on my desk.

Gitmo's swings came faster, hitting just about anything that was labeled an employee benefit. Unfortunately for me, the State Employee Relations Department had purchased box seats and they were in the third row with plastic megaphones blasting cheers for Gitmo. Unpaid benefits were one hard punch that sent me spinning. I noticed my D-T-I score had dropped a few points to 1.05 on the stadium D-T-I score board.

I was determined not to let this get to me. I kept my guard up and my arms close to my side. I pivoted and gave him a hard right by verifying all of our unpaid benefits. I quickly countered with a left and a plan to reduce all unpaid benefit debt to the lowest agreed-to amounts. Health benefits were paid first.

Gitmo's chin sank. I was becoming more comfortable in the ring. The loud noise of the cheering crowd somehow moved to the background. My full concentration took over.

Next, I began to chip away at our accrued vacation time. I announced a use-it-or-lose-it policy. I compared all unpaid vacation time and benefits against existing time cards. Suddenly, from out of nowhere, I received a light blow to the head when I discovered that a few benefits were not accurately reported. My unpaid overtime showed a lower debt than the employees actually reported. In one instance, the employee's benefits were actually higher than the report showed. I had overlooked some reported overtime on one of her time cards.

I didn't waste any time in correcting the issue. The debt from the total unpaid benefits was adjusted, which quickly improved my score. Even when I added the difference to the company's debt, the adjustments were still in our favor.

Back-to-back with this move, I countered Gitmo by getting agreements for vacation schedules and required that benefits be taken within specific time frames. This allowed me to reduce the company's debt to exactly match the employees' reported benefit numbers.

My return jab threw Gitmo into a whirl. Once I positively knew that my unpaid benefits were accurate, I gave each employee a formal written agreement and put it on file. The three right-left returns hit Gitmo square in the nose.

My D-T-I lifted from .01 to 1.00 even, and I finally came out of the Seedling "hobby" phase, advancing to a Startup. Just then the bell rang, and we both headed to our corners for the end of Round 1.

Round 2: THE STARTUP:
"Drawing The Early Punch"

D-T-I   1.01 - 1.09

The short break flew by quickly. Mr. Kanketa wiped the sweat off my forehead and switched out my chewed mouthguard. I was displaying a few bruises, but there was nothing too serious at this point. The second round is usually where the tide changes. "You are my sunshine . . . my only sunshine," I chanted to myself. Then the bell to open Round 2 pierced my ears.

I hurried out of the startup gate and back into the ring.

Gitmo Debt had no intention of playing fair in this one. He came out swinging hard.

First, he threw a sharp jab at my unpaid taxes. His quick sequence of lunges were really painful. I was dizzy. He walloped my eye pretty hard. There were both unpaid federal and state sales and use taxes in limbo with high interest and high penalties accruing. I noticed that this was really taking a toll on my D-T-I score. Had I wasted even a minute more I was sure to get liens, which would prevent me from getting loans and the match would be over—in Gitmo Debt's favor, of course. I snapped back with an offer in compromise tax payment plan to the feds and a payment plan to the state. I would have to pay these over time as long-term debts, but every time I made another payment, my debt balance would drop slightly.

To make matters worse, over the roar of the crowd, some guy in the auditorium yelled out, "Hey, you promised me a kickback for our purchase volume last year. Did you forget?" The crowd jeered. For a split second, Gitmo Debt had me. Yes, it was my verbal agreement to pay him finder's fees on jobs.

The response flew out of my mouth. "This Friday!" I yelled back. "This Friday, man. Paid this Friday!" I added him to the unpaid debts list.

The sales guy was wrong about one thing. I never use the word "kickback." It's legally dangerous. I would also deny making any verbal promises for stock to any supplier or salesperson because I happened to be swarming with guilt about late payments.

Gitmo's assistant, Seymour Corts, would attack me under oath about casual promises for stock and a "piece of the action." Gitmo knows that these types of promises are legitimate debts. Nonetheless, the unpaid commissions sent me hard to the mat. The room was spinning and my ears were ringing as I heard the ref counting.

I was back on my knees at the count of five, but I can't deny that I was feeling it. I was low on cash and admittedly, I did put off some of the supplier promises I made. But luck was on my side. Fortunately for me, there were some unspent deposits in transit that I could factor.

I managed to recover by setting up a payment plan with the sales guy. It didn't help my D-T-I much, but I did manage to get to 1.11 before the round was over.

The bell didn't come too soon, and again we each retreated to our respective corners.

Round 3: CRITICAL RECOVERY
"A Dangerous Moment"

ROUND 3

D-T-I   1.10 - 1.24

I was proud of my accomplishments so far, but round by round it was nothing less than agonizing. I sat on the stool, trying hard to recover. My breathing was heavy, short, and sporadic. It felt a lot like a bad case of asthma. Mr. Kanketa was applying wraps to my bruised rib cage.

"Mr. K., the rounds seem to be going from bad to worse. My D-T-I is spiking up and down with every Gitmo swing."

Kanketa gave me a much needed word of encouragement. "But when you look at your D-T-I trend, overall your average points are steadily increasing. You're doing good. Don't give up now. Keep 'er going!"

By this time I had really worked up a sweat, and a thirst to match. I knew it would take more than a sip of Gatorade to move necessary recovery in my business life cycle.

Barry Deeply was busy patting down Gitmo's head with cold, wet towels as he funneled coaching tips into Gitmo's pig ears. I observed that I had inflicted a few deep cuts that I didn't see earlier. The clang of the bell pumped new energy into my being. Again we moved into the ring, and the fighting began within seconds.

Gitmo came at me briskly with a side punch of some non-cancelable purchase orders that I had from our customers. They were

127

undelivered debts, and they wreaked havoc on our D-T-I. Thankfully, I had longstanding relationships with some of the customers and I was able to negotiate these debts by adding in cancelation clauses with more reasonable terms and with a lower penalty if we couldn't deliver. I spread out the project delivery time and got the customers to agree to smaller deliveries.

In some cases, I had to job out projects that we would normally have taken, just to offload some of the debt. The contracts were revised, and Gitmo's return hits were lighter than I anticipated.

D-T-I was now hovering around 1.19. I needed six more points to win the round. I was still in Critical Recovery.

Gitmo hit me furiously square on, aiming again at my right rib cage, then following with a strike to my torso. This time, he came at me with his reliably damaging unearned income punch. I glanced over at Mr. Kanketa. He knew what I was thinking. He put me on high alert with his eyes.

For a host of reasons, customer prepayments are simply dangerous, and Barry Deeply was coaching Gitmo to play that card.

Just then, Seymour Corts, Bill's assistant, yelled at the referee from the sideline, "Hey, ref, did you know that the law points to contractor theft if they spend customer money without doing work?" The referee blew the whistle and came over to me.

"What's this? Are you are spending customer unearned income?"

I was being stonewalled. Just this week, two of my customers prepaid us for a job. I'd already spent half of the money on payroll, and we hadn't started on the work yet. At that moment, I found myself in a really tough spot. I knew I needed to tighten up on my customer policies for spending money on projects. I knew I couldn't show proof of delivery. Unearned income is not just any old debt. It's legally dangerous, and it could have whirled me back to a Startup position. We'd be bankrupt. I had to be nimble.

I hollered back loudly at the ref so that Seymour could hear: "I just sent a note to my employees to drop everything and concentrate on completing the projects that we had down payments for! As we complete each group of steps, I am sending each customer a time-stamped email of the status of their job and the percentage of the work completed! I am also including a notice that I bought supplies!"

The referee grabbed the microphone and over the sound system, made the announcement. His cutting voice penetrated the crowd.

"You have until the end of this round to make progress on your unearned income or your D-T-I score will bounce back to less than 1.00. Do you know what that means?"

I nodded my head with acknowledgement. I shuddered to think I would bounce back to a Seedling. That would be bankruptcy and the game would be over.

Time was running down on the clock. Gitmo and I exchanged extreme punches. Then, a runner slipped a message to the ref. It was just in the nick of time. My team had just completed the work percentages that totaled the spent down payment amounts. Every completed phase became earned income and reduced my debt by the earned amount.

The bell went off and I had managed to keep my D-T-I score in place. The added finished project work planted my D-T-I right where I wanted it at 1.25. It was a really close call.

Round 4: NECESSARY RECOVERY
"It'll Take Some Fancy Footwork"

ROUND 4

D-T-I   1.25 - 1.49

The next D-T-I goal of 1.49 demanded some fancy footwork on my part. I had a little relief from moving out of the Critical Recovery D-T-I range. I knew I had to get through Necessary Recovery quickly. Mr. Kanketa would always say, "The longer you sit in one D-T-I range, the longer it takes to move out of it."

Mr. Kanketa pulled off my right glove to tighten my wrapped hand. A fierce determination grabbed me. I had saved a new reinvestment deposit and was ready to use it for business growth.

"Hold it," Mr. Kanketa pressed me. "Don't spend reinvestment money to grow the business in this D-T-I range. Chewing up all of your profit trying to grow too quickly is exactly what Gitmo wants you to do. You need to conserve your energy and your cash wherever possible. Right now, the business is out of balance. Fix the business problems first, before you reinvest for growth."

Kanketa's coaching didn't come too soon. I was really close to randomly spending for things I was not sure would get me a 2-to-1 return. It was only guesswork. At that moment, guesswork at this low cash level would not be good enough for a win.

"Gitmo's showing early signs of fatigue," Kanketa pointed out. "Hold back on all new expenses as long as you can. Keep up your guard, and hold your position as long as possible. Duck every temptation to grow the business right now. Let him spend all of his reserve energy.

Wait until your D-T-I hits 1.49. Then give him an all-out punch and shove your business to the next level."

There's the bell. Into the ring we went.

Gitmo was unable to conceal his number one weakness. He's a short-termer, with out-of-the-gate brute strength, but almost no stamina. He would have little sustainability from a diligent opponent who was trained in long-term tactics. When he saw that I was keeping up with him, he backed off of the reinvestment angle. He had to drive me some other way. He went for trade debt. Trade payables debt was a little strategy that Gitmo used when he wanted to interrupt growth.

He first threw me a slow left with some unpaid Cost of Goods suppliers. He suspected I would always pay the loudest screamers. During our training, Kanketa had coached me masterfully to prioritize our suppliers as either critical, necessary, or helpful to our business. Too often I would pay the helpful suppliers who screamed the loudest.

"Begin by only negotiating with non-critical suppliers," Kanketa said. "Then, isolate your CODs from your overdue debt amount."

My glove went up over my face, and my D-T-I shot up from 1.25 all the way to 1.32. I was gaining points.

Round 4 was very strenuous. Gitmo faked me out and repeatedly swiped me with some general unpaid operational bills.

"Yikes! Now what?" Mr. K. was within earshot. "I am slipping and hurting my credit score by paying non-people costs late. And no line of credit is making matters worse!"

"Quick. Stop the bleeding. Go for factoring, which you should temporarily use as your line of credit. Pay as many of your fixed, unpaid, non-people operational costs as possible . . . anything that isn't a person, with your factoring tool!" Mr. Kanketa ranted.

We'd talked about this in training. Almost everyone who can't get a line of credit qualifies for factoring, and the interest rate is generally very reasonable. I'd heard that factoring is a good temporary fix because you get your late-paying customer money in a day or two and your customers can still lag on their payments. I called a factoring company and signed up. "You can continue to factor, but I recommend that you also get a line of credit when your business heals. Once your new line of credit is in place, don't touch your deposits for the entire month. Let all of your deposits for the month accumulate in your business checkbook. Then, on the last day of the month, pay off everything, including your line of credit, with your bank deposits. All that's left is your net profit. Each new month follows the same contour. Repeat, repeat, repeat."

I paid off some of the more critical non-people suppliers with my factoring deposit just in time to beat the bell.

Before I knew it, Round 4 was over.

Round 5: THE ORGANIC PUNCH
"Debt From Within"

ROUND 3

D-T-I   1.50 - 1.99

There I sat. All I can say is the stool felt good on my rear end and God bless those Gatorade specialists. I was weary, but energized. With my D-T-I now at 1.52, my enthusiastic fans cheered me. With my great trainer and coach, I was out in front and pulling ahead. I popped up from my stool—and that's the last thing I remember.

I shouldn't have started out so overconfidently. I know for sure that the bell rang because there I was, laying on the coarse rubber mat. I had blanked out. For a moment, it seemed like I was a real goner. It felt like I was laying on the mat for an hour. The jeers in the crowd woke me up. The lights blinded me. Through my bruised left eye, I saw Gitmo walking to center circle with his big arms in the air, clasping his hands in victory. The thunderous noise of the crowd was primarily hissing and booing.

What the hell happened? Was it over? Did I lose? Then I heard the ref counting off. "Shadow debts, six; shadow debts, seven; shadow debts, eight . . ." and realized that I had to get up under all circumstances. Dazed and dumbfounded, I pushed myself up with my elbows and struggled to my feet and hobbled over to the ref.

"Shadow payables, ref? Are you kidding me?" I squawked.

Loans from friends and family were never in my business equation. He gnarled back, "Learn the rules, buddy, or get out of the game!" The tone of his voice assured me that he wasn't messing around. The boos of the crowd blatantly revealed their displeasure at the call. But, as you already know, the complaints didn't affect the ref's decision one iota.

Along the way, I needed money for the business and the banks weren't being cooperative. My decision to go within or go without ended up with Mom and Dad, who first stepped up and loaned the business money from their life's savings. I had other friends who were happy to do the same. All in all, the debt amount was significant. In fact, shadow debt was easily a quarter of all of our debt. I just didn't look at family loans as company debt.

I couldn't see myself in court with my kind and supportive family and friends suing me. Yet, my shadow payables were nonetheless an inarguable part of our business debt. Who knows what circumstances would change the tide and catch me blindsided with the most trusted people in my life? When would my guilt hold me ransom when they needed money for their own health situations, or perhaps assisted living? Where would my loyalty be if it came down to family and friends or the company? How would an estate handle the loans? What happens when I sell the business down the road and now my friends ask the new owner for their money?

This round was strenuous. As I totaled these shadow debts and added them to my debts page, I watched the D-T-I score that I'd worked so hard for slam me back to 1.23—Critical Recovery.

Besides the money itself, which was unrecorded, much of the problem was the way it was handled. Mom, bless her heart, wrote checks directly to my company instead of loaning to me personally. It would have been much better had she written them directly to me to loan into the company. It was a sudden jolt to my system and frankly, quite a mess.

Needless to say, Gitmo, Barry, and Seymour were overjoyed, and were getting ready to throw a victory party. There was one last knuckle punch that I'd learned in Kanketa's training. I decided to cash in all my receivables and go for total factoring of all receivables beyond 30 days. Before Gitmo Debt had a chance to return another blow, I took the factored money and paid off a major portion of the debt. The total would cover all but about $10,000 of the shadow debts. The family and my friends were appreciative, and I noticed sighs of relief when I gave them the money.

My D-T-I spiked to 1.84. "Whew! That was one damn close call!" Kanketa yelled. "But you're not quite done. Finish it off with the proper paperwork for the loan balances!"

I knew what he was saying. Mom and Dad formally forgave their other unpaid $5,000 in writing, which put D-T-I at 2.03 and I wrote up a small, interest-bearing agreement to my friend for the other $5,000. The bell sounded, and Round 5 was history.

Round 6: THE POINT OF ACQUISITION
"When In Doubt, Try Sparring"

ROUND 6

D-T-I   2.00 - 2.49

My patience in my training paid off in spades. Gitmo was losing and he knew it.

Round 6 was going to be equally challenging. Gitmo was still standing, and he was playing dirty. This time, he delivered a big whack to my kisser. Loans payable to owners was his slug of the day.

There was the loud bell, followed by Gitmo's deliberate belt. Once again, I toppled hard to the rubber surface. I heard the count of four before I could bring myself to my feet. Barry Deeply was surely behind this one.

Honestly? It wasn't a pretty picture. There were unidentified loans that I'd made to the company that I completely forgot about. There were also various paychecks that I didn't personally take, dating back two years. There were loans from checks that I directly deposited written to the company from people who loaned me money. There was money I took out to pay myself from money I thought I loaned in. What a mess!

It seemed like, and felt like, loans to company by the owner was another quarter of our total debt. I was unnecessarily paying a lot of taxes. I just couldn't prove a damn thing. Nothing had paperwork.

If only. If only I had done things right as I was doing them. If only. If only. "Mr. Kanketa. What now?" I petitioned.

"The last thing you need is to go down fighting while you're still fixing. Sparring is making the motions of boxing without landing heavy blows. Move and miss without mashing. You need to buy time."

Buying time was one thing I could do expertly. My sparring antics caught Gitmo off guard. He swung. He missed. He swung. He missed. I was pulsing him and it was wearing him down.

"Mr. Kanketa!" I squealed. "So, how do I fix this mess quickly?"

Kanketa had answers for everything, until now. "You can't!" he thundered.

My eyes rolled back in my head. "I can't what?"

"There isn't a quick fix!"

"Ughh! Are you joking? Am I licked?"

"No. But you have to really pay attention to every move. Only absolute, full concentration will be your friend that will save you!"

I was still sparring, and Gitmo was plainly bone-tired, but his swings were still inches too close for comfort. I treasure the shape of my nose. During Round 6, Kanketa was coaching me through the fix from the other side of the ropes. I found myself bouncing off the heavy, spring-lined ropes more during this round than any other. Sweat poured from every angstrom of my head. Needless to say, sparring while fixing was a tough multi-tasking assignment.

I had to create interest-bearing loan agreements between me personally and the company for every loan I wanted to count. There were seven in all. I was grateful when the total debt to the company for my loans was less than I thought. It could have been much, much worse. But the loans still needed to be official. If I wanted to keep my D-T-I of 2.03, I would have to capitalize the company. In other words, my loans would no longer be loans, but investments. I wouldn't be able to repay myself now, but later, my company stock could be potentially worth more. Gitmo didn't like that move in the least.

I was just signing the last of my loan agreements as the bell resonantly tolled. On to Round 7.

Round 7: TRANSFER OF POWER
"Down For The Count"

ROUND 7

D-T-I   2.50 - 3.99

During the break, I propped myself up in the corner, my elbows wrapped around the tightly weaved rope corners of the ring. Round by round, my recovery time was longer than the previous round, but my D-T-I was holding at a strong 2.64. It was no secret that my business acumen was still tainted with some weak spots. I had unpaid, high-interest loans with large payments and big balances. Since I had used up all my factorable receivables between 30 and 89 days to pay off my shadow debts back in Round 5, I now found myself low on cash without enough immediate receivables available for my loan payments. I was once again dancing in the danger zone if the lenders called their loans in. To survive this hit, I had to manage the loans better or the round would not go well. My instincts took over.

At the bong of the brass, I sprang into the ring with some fancy footwork. The first thing I did was to separate our short-term loans from long-term loans and focus on those short-term folks who needed to be paid back in twelve months or less.

"Hey, Mr. K.! What should I budget for all of my short-term loans?"

His feedback was very specific. "Never, never more than 12.5% of your total profit." It was more than a casual remark. His experience clung to every word.

"Standard short-term business loans are from non-owner sources such as banks, investment companies, credit cards, and other lenders. Reorganize the total of all your current loan payments to outside lenders so that you stay within 12.5% of last year's net profit. It's on your last year's Profit and Loss Statement."

"That's a weird formula. Never heard that one before!" I sassed.

I was trying to listen and box with Gitmo at the same time.

"Hey . . . how do I calculate this again?"

"Divide last year's total sales by twelve to get your monthly sales average!" Kanketa wailed.

"Next, subtract your last year's cost of goods sold average from your annual sales average to get last year's average monthly margin. We haven't got time. I'll explain later! Right now, just use the average monthly margin from last year multiplied by .042. It's the same number as the 12.5% of net profit. Get all of your short-term loans to add up to this amount every month. Fight like hell to get this to happen!"

In the middle of the round with Gitmo I was hardly in a position to refute this. I had no experience, and Kanketa's answer was my best shot. I had no choice but to trust it.

"Good enough for me!" I screeched.

Gitmo tripped me as the ref looked away. I fell on my right knee. "Ouch!" I cried in pain. My money was casually loaned into the company with no formal agreements in place. In fact, I had no idea how much my company owed me for declining to take my full paycheck for the first two years. Guesswork was clearly not going to be acceptable. Fortunately, as owner, I was in a flexible position to remove my own debts with a swift entry into the minutes of our quarterly meeting.

I converted what I knew of my loans to capital investments. With no actual proof of the debt totals, it didn't feel good, but for the moment, I was at least able to hold my D-T-I score in place at 3.54. I had an American Express card that was due every month. I had a Capital One loan that was finally due in a few months. There was also a bank loan balance to be fully paid in the current year. When I added them up, the total exceeded the formula by $1,400.

The clock was running out and I had to think on my feet. I called the banks and extended our payments another 16 months to reduce $800 of the payment. I had $600 to go before I was in balance with Kanketa's formula.

I was able to inch up to 3.98 by paying off some of the bank and credit card debt with what was available in my factored receivables account. This put my budget into balance. I negotiated some short-term loans with non-critical suppliers to extend beyond 13 weeks.

I gave Gitmo a swift hard left, striking at his jaw. Fortunately, he had two chins, resembling my punching bags, which made the target easier. I temporarily used money from my tax budget to pay off the rest of the balance. Taxes wouldn't come due until the end of the year and technically, there wasn't a specific tax debt in place yet. I had time to replace my tax money. Financial balance was more important to the match.

Round 8: VICTIM TO VICTOR
"The Final 4:1 Blow"

ROUND 8

D-T-I 4.00 +

I had a feeling this would be my last round.

My eyes were fixed on Gitmo in the opposite corner. Barry Deeply kept taking his pulse. Seymour was worthless. He was expressionless as we calmly drank down Gitmo's Gatorade cooler.

Gitmo was sprawled out on the stool and his bloated belly hung over the edge, keeping half of the stool legs from sight. He was breathing hard and had severely puffy eyes. He clearly wouldn't withstand another round. At the clang of the bell, I made a decision. It was time to finish off old Gitmo for good.

The trophy number was 4.00. After this, I wouldn't have to be too concerned with D-T-I. It was only maintenance from there forward. As long as I maintained this score, I could be absent from my business for months at a time and the business would continue to hold its highest value.

"Mr. K., I still have a couple of long-term debts to get in line. I added up my long-term tax monthly payments, the offer in compromise, and the payment plan to the state to my three-year loan for a roof repair on our building that has a high monthly payment. I had also financed office equipment, primarily computers, over 24 months. Do you have a reliable formula for this?"

"Use the same formula of .042 of monthly margin average for both long-term and short-term!" he called back.

"Step with the lead foot and drag the rear foot. Your weight is grounded and you maintain balance, always ready to attack or defend. Get all of your maximum long-term loan payments to match your maximum short-term payments. Then take your final punch at Gitmo and knock his lights out!"

I did just that. The final blow came to Gitmo when I refinanced my two long-term loans and the monthly payments balanced each other at 12.5%. The shortcut secret was the .042 of last year's margin average. I could have used either. It was excellent advice and the final punch I was waiting for.

Gitmo Debt staggered, whirled, and fell flat on his face. He lay there and wasn't moving. The ref finished to the count of ten. Just then, the phoenix arose from the ashes. It was a moment of ecstasy. I won! For a minute, I thought I was related to everyone in the stadium. It looked like each and every person in the crowd was hugging with joy.

I won for my family. I won for the company. I won for everyone who came to support me. It was my victory that would be remembered for years to come.

It was certainly a difficult match, but infinitely well worth it. All the cuts, scrapes, and bruises would heal over time. The flashes from the photographers were blinding. The ref held my hand high in the air. I was a champion. Someone handed me a shiny trophy with a brush-polished faceplate that read:

D-T-I Champion

At that moment, I vowed to never again relinquish my title to any future challengers of Income and Debt.

CHAPTER 8

KEEP YOUR GLOVES HANDY

After the fight, there was the presentation of the trophy for my well-earned D-T-I score. I was shuttled back to a dressing room by security. Photographers were pushing their way through the exuberant crowd that hugged the doorway. Somehow, I managed to wedge myself into the room. The security guards closed the door tightly behind me. With my damp towel still clinging to my neck, I spun around to head to my locker.

There he was. My elegant trainer, Mr. Kanketa. His fedora was tight on his head, and a glint of jubilance embellished the corners of his eyes.

"Congratulations are in order," he said. "You did it!"

I was speechless with gratitude. "Yes, we did it," I finally replied. "We did it."

"So, what's next?" he quizzed.

"Next? Well, from what I can see, I guess there will be another match. Gitmo lost this one, but he isn't going to just walk away licking his wounds."

"No, but he will think twice about investing a lot of effort into a well-prepared contender."

"All I can say is this fight was a grand success."

"Success? Really? How do you define success?" he asked.

I laughed heartily. "That's pretty easy. When you get what you want, that's success."

He smiled and calmly offered another rendition. "Perhaps in many circles that would be one definition that might be often used."

I asked him in surprise, "Well, then, how else could you possibly define it?"

"To me, success isn't having what you want. Success is not having what you don't want. You might not have all of the revenue you want right now, but if you are able to get rid of the debt you don't want, and keep your business and your family safe, which is what you do want, in my book, you are a huge success." His words were insightful.

By then, the clamoring outside the room had escalated. I went to the door and peeked through the crack. I saw my family and friends and all of those who were affected by my D-T-I score among the horde, waving at me. They were beaming with pride.

When I turned back to the room, Mr. Kanketa had left. He had ducked out unnoticed. I could hardly blame him. I was tired, and would certainly catch up with him in the morning.

It was late, and the high-pitched volume of the enthusiastic crowd had quieted considerably. The stadium cleared and many left, trying to avoid the congestion in the parking lot. Security was no longer needed, and the guards also slipped away quietly. I reached down to unwrap my hands, which were still tightly clenched. The long stretch wraps fell off easily. My hands still ached from the tight grip I had been holding for an unknown amount of time.

I slowly opened my right palm to find a small, pink piece of paper, doubly folded, that I held tightly in my clasp. It was the Gitmo sticky note that Susan, my bookkeeper, had put on the accounts receivable page weeks before. I noticed her scribble. It read: "The journey begins here."

She was right. Perhaps this was the biggest fight, and it might not be my last. It certainly wasn't everything I needed to know about my business, but it was more than enough to become a champion. I now know how to bring down Gitmo Debt.

I exchanged my boxing attire for the clothes I had worn to the office. Our home wasn't far from the arena and I made it in ten minutes.

The house was quiet and the lights were out. Sarah and the kids were already in bed. I wondered if anyone remembered to feed the fish. I made myself a tuna on rye and poured a glass of orange juice. Then I slowly pulled up one of the wooden stools near the island in the kitchen, where I sat quietly in thought.

I was proud of myself. I followed my gut and trusted my instincts. All in all, Mr. Kanketa taught me twelve good moves that would last me for as long as I own a business.

In the weeks ahead, I started to swing with D-T-I. When I finally began operating from the real truth about my business, I got it under control. Our business changed quickly in ways and for reasons I can't explain. I went from the sidelines to the center ring and commanded a champion's respect.

Our customers began to pay more quickly. Our suppliers were more timely, friendlier, better mannered, and seemed to be putting a little more effort into serving us. Employees were much happier and generously filled the suggestion box, making it a routine part of their week. Even the banks were buying us box office seats at local events and throwing in dinners here and there. All because of a little knowledge.

With my new crystal ball, I could finally see into the future. There it was. My shiny, polished financial freedom trophy, sitting in full view, waiting for me to pick it up whenever I choose.

The week after my Fight Night, I got Mr. Kanketa's final bill. Needless to say, I paid it promptly. In the envelope, he left a small card. I took it over to the printer and had it blown up to poster size.

It's hanging on our wall today.

DECLINING

DTI

SHOULD

BE AVOIDED

Robbing you of time and money

Stealing your company's value

Shrinking your future

Unnecessary stress

All thanks to Mr. Kanketa, for the first time in nearly two years, I could honestly say, "I used to hate my business. Now, I love it."

Any and all logos and references to companies
that appear in this book are the property
and registered trademarks of those companies.
Kanketa and its business units have
no current affiliation with the companies
appearing in this material.

D-T-I CASE STUDY

YEAR ONE

The Duvall Company was saddled with a heavy debt load. When they began to track D-T-I, the company was not bankable. The first D-T-I score was .55 (.55 cents of income to pay every $1.00 of debt). In other words, they were bankrupt, and in a Seedling position.

With their target of .10 improvement per month (.05 debt reduction and .05 income increase), they created a D-T-I 4-year forecast (left panel below).

Target Goal: 4:1

In a perfect world they would achieve their target goal of 4:1 D-T-I in 12 months

(circled in year 3 projections; left panel below).

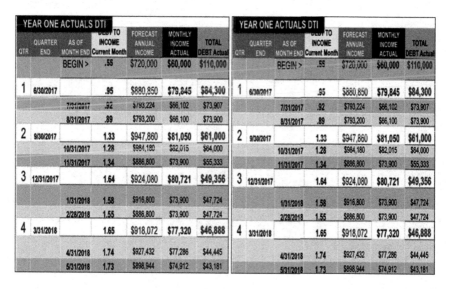

QTR	QUARTER END	AS OF MONTH END	DEBT TO INCOME Current Month	FORECAST ANNUAL INCOME	MONTHLY INCOME ACTUAL	TOTAL DEBT Actual
		BEGIN >	.55	$720,000	$60,000	$110,000
1	6/30/2017		.95	$880,850	$79,845	$84,300
		7/31/2017	.92	$793,224	$66,102	$73,907
		8/31/2017	.89	$793,200	$66,100	$73,900
2	9/30/2017		1.33	$947,860	$81,050	$61,000
		10/31/2017	1.28	$984,180	$82,015	$64,000
		11/31/2017	1.34	$886,800	$73,900	$55,333
3	12/31/2017		1.64	$924,080	$80,721	$49,356
		1/31/2018	1.58	$916,800	$73,900	$47,724
		2/28/2018	1.55	$886,800	$73,900	$47,724
4	3/31/2018		1.65	$918,072	$77,320	$46,888
		4/31/2018	1.74	$927,432	$77,286	$44,445
		5/31/2018	1.73	$898,944	$74,912	$43,181

QTR	QUARTER END	AS OF MONTH END	DEBT TO INCOME Current Month	FORECAST ANNUAL INCOME	MONTHLY INCOME ACTUAL	TOTAL DEBT Actual
		BEGIN >	.55	$720,000	$60,000	$110,000
1	6/30/2017		.95	$880,850	$79,845	$84,300
		7/31/2017	.92	$793,224	$66,102	$73,907
		8/31/2017	.89	$793,200	$66,100	$73,900
2	9/30/2017		1.33	$947,860	$81,050	$61,000
		10/31/2017	1.28	$984,180	$82,015	$64,000
		11/31/2017	1.34	$886,800	$73,900	$55,333
3	12/31/2017		1.64	$924,080	$80,721	$49,356
		1/31/2018	1.58	$916,800	$73,900	$47,724
		2/28/2018	1.55	$886,800	$73,900	$47,724
4	3/31/2018		1.65	$918,072	$77,320	$46,888
		4/31/2018	1.74	$927,432	$77,286	$44,445
		5/31/2018	1.73	$898,944	$74,912	$43,181

YEAR ONE ACTUALS DTI

Actual

Because the world is not perfect, the panel on the right reflects what really happened.

Both sides share the same begin date, the same starting income and debt. By the end of the first 90 days (6/30/2017 above), following some education, setup time, and a few practice runs, Duvall was ahead of their 90-day projection by .10 (.95 on right panel).

YEAR TWO

Despite their awareness of their target D-T-I monthly and quarterly goals (left panel), the Duvall Company suffered several mishaps in the business during the second year.

It was necessary to increase debt to repair a damaged roof and buy new software to keep competitive.

The D-T-I fluctuated somewhat. However, as you can see in the right panel, an upward D-T-I trend kept the company's health in check, and 2:1 was generally maintained while the industry experienced a severe downturn overall.

YEAR TWO TARGET DTI

QTR	QUARTER END	MONTH END	DEBT TO INCOME	TARGET ANNUAL INCOME	MONTHLY INCOME	TOTAL DEBT NOT TO EXCEED
5	6/30/2018		2.05	$945,000	$95,937	$46,903
		7/31/2018	2.15		$98,333	$45,833
		8/31/2018	2.25		$100,729	$44,833
6	9/30/2018		2.35	$990,000	$103,125	$43,968
		10/30/2018	2.45		$105,521	$43,150
		11/31/2017	2.55		$107,917	$42,396
7	12/31/2018		2.65	$1,035,000	$110,313	$41,699
		1/31/2019	2.75		$112,708	$41,053
		2/28/2019	2.85		$115,104	$40,452
8	3/31/2019		2.95	$1,080,000	$117,500	$39,892
		4/31/2019	3.05		$119,896	$39,369
		5/31/2019	3.15		$122,292	$38,879

YEAR TWO ACTUALS DTI

QTR	QUARTER END	AS OF MONTH END	DEBT TO INCOME Current Month	FORECAST ANNUAL INCOME	MONTHLY INCOME ACTUAL	TOTAL DEBT Actual
5	6/30/2018		1.92	$944,888	$81,050	$42,131
		7/31/2018	1.98	$975,240	$81,270	$41,000
		8/31/2018	2.04	$886,824	$73,902	$36,307
6	9/30/2018		2.27	$933,128	$79,387	$35,022
		10/31/2018	2.33	$994,620	$82,885	$35,022
		11/30/2018	2.11	$852,120	$71,013	$33,718
7	12/31/2018		2.55	$913,996	$84,010	$32,909
		1/31/2019	2.33	$880,908	$73,409	$31,534
		2/28/2019	2.37	$852,960	$71,080	$30,020
8	3/31/2019		2.97	$1,018,564	$85,320	$28,712
		4/31/201	2.83	$1,010,172	$84,182	$29,750
		5/31/2019	2.83	$1,021,680	$85,140	$30,123

YEAR THREE

As the industry slowly rebounded during year three, a solid upward D-T-I trend gave the Duvall Company a leading edge.

They gained a sound financial footing and found themselves in a position to take on large projects and new customer opportunities. The 4:1 D-T-I goal appeared in the year 3 forecast (left panel below).

While the company missed the target, it was in good financial shape and improving the D-T-I monthly. The banks were very receptive to factoring and cash flow loans as needed.

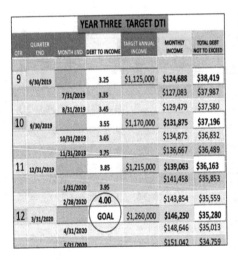

	YEAR THREE TARGET DTI				
QTR	QUARTER END	MONTH END	TARGET ANNUAL DEBT TO INCOME	MONTHLY INCOME	TOTAL DEBT NOT TO EXCEED
9	6/30/2019		3.25	$1,125,000 $124,688	$38,419
		7/31/2019	3.35	$127,083	$37,987
		8/31/2019	3.45	$129,479	$37,580
10	9/30/2019		3.55	$1,170,000 $131,875	$37,196
		10/31/2019	3.65	$134,875	$36,832
		11/31/2019	3.75	$136,667	$36,489
11	12/31/2019		3.85	$1,215,000 $139,063	$36,163
		1/31/2020	3.95	$141,458	$35,853
		2/28/2020	4.00 GOAL	$143,854	$35,559
12	3/31/2020			$1,260,000 $146,250	$35,280
		4/31/2020		$148,646	$35,013
		5/31/2020		$151,042	$34,759

	YEAR THREE ACTUALS DTI		DEBT TO INCOME Current Month	FORECAST ANNUAL INCOME	MONTHLY INCOME ACTUAL	TOTAL DEBT Actual
QTR	QUARTER END	AS OF MONTH END				
9	6/30/2019		2.78	$1,020,440	$81,050	$29,160
		7/31/2019	3.12	$1,052,676	$87,723	$28,116
		8/31/2019	3.19	$1,036,320	$86,360	$27,060
10	9/30/2019		2.83	$979,220	$80,225	$28,365
		10/31/2019	3.19	$1,015,764	$84,647	$26,566
		11/30/2019	3.03	$959,196	$79,933	$26,403
11	12/31/2019		2.86	$1,065,792	$83,371	$29,111
		1/31/2020	3.14	$1,069,200	$89,100	$28,403
		2/28/2020	2.52	$1,127,724	$93,977	$37,274
12	3/31/2020		3..02	$1,015,852	$87,715	$29,088
		4/31/2020	3.00	$1,047,432	$87,286	$28,411
		5/31/2020	2.00	$947,544	$78,962	$26,345

YEAR FOUR

The Duvall Company achieved 4:1 and had acquired two competitors.

Mr. Duvall made a choice to work a little less, while the company remained safe and continued to grow in his absence.

QTR	QUARTER END	MONTH END	DEBT TO INCOME	TARGET ANNUAL INCOME	MONTHLY INCOME	TOTAL DEBT NOT TO EXCEED
13	6/30/2020			$1,305,000	$153,438	$34,516
		7/31/2020			$155,833	$34,283
		8/31/2020			$158,229	$34,061
14	9/30/2020			$1,350,000	$160,625	$33,848
		10/31/2020			$163,021	$33,644
		11/30/2020			$165,417	$33,448
15	12/31/2020			$1,395,000	$167,813	$33,260
		1/31/2021			$170,208	$33,079
		2/28/2021			$72,604	$32,905
16	3/31/2021			$1,440,000	$175,000	$32,738
		4/31/2021			$177,500	$32,596
		5/31/2021			$180,000	$32,459

FOUR YEAR TARGET DTI

YEAR FOUR ACTUALS DTI

QTR	QUARTER END	AS OF MONTH END	DEBT TO INCOME Current Month	FORECAST ANNUAL INCOME	MONTHLY INCOME ACTUAL	TOTAL DEBT Actual
13	6/30/2020		3.48	$1,143,812	$81,050	$23,298
		7/31/2020	4.11	$1,033,151	$101,000	$24,600
		8/31/2020	3.90	$866,574	$103,903	$26,666
14	9/30/2020		3.28	$1,107,872	$81,050	$24,677
		10/31/2020	3.43	784,584	$91,000	$26,519
		11/31/2020	3.58	$567,739	$104,918	$29,318
15	12/31/2020		3.88	$1,146,680	$93,050	$23,975
		1/31/2021	4.31	$959,927	$95,720	$22,222
		2/28/2021	4.06	$743,027	$97,900	$24,112
16	3/31/2021	ACTUAL		$1,218,912	$96,115	$22,945
		4/31/2021		$1,163,096	$109,700	$22,112
		5/31/2021		$922,777	$98,913	$22,482

Debt Form

PAYABLES DEBT	LAST MONTH's DEBT	THIS MONTH PAYABLES DEBT REDUCTION	PAYABLES BALANCE NEXT MONTH BEGIN
1. ACCRUED PAYROLL Unpaid Wages	$	$	$
2. ACCRUED PAYROLL Unpaid Benefits	$	$	$
3. TRADE PAYABLES	$	$	$
4. NON-CANCELABLE POs w. penalties	$	$	$
5. PREPAYMENTS FROM CUSTOMERS	$	$	$
6. UNPAID OVERHEAD EXPENSES	$	$	$
7. SHADOW PAYABLES	$	$	$
8. COMMISSIONS DUE	$	$	$
9. LOANS PAYABLE TO OWNERS	$	$	$
10 UNPAID TAXES (all)	$	$	$
11 CURRENT LOANS non-owner (12 mo. or less)	$	$	$
12 TERM LOANS non-owner (13 mo.+)	$	$	$
TOTALS	$	$	$

Income Form

INCOME	ROW TOTALS	NOTE:
1. CHECKING ACCOUNT DEPOSITS and CASH ON HAND	$	
2. DEPOSITS IN TRANSIT	$	
3. SAVINGS and INVESTMENTS	$	
4. ACCNTS RECEIVABLE 1-30 days	$	
5. ACCNTS RECEIVABLE 31-60 days	$	
6. ACCNTS RECEIVABLE 61-89 days	$	
7. ACCNTS FACTORED, NOT REDEEMED	$	
8. NON CANCELABLE PURCHASE ORDERS (with penalties)	$	
9. UNPAID LOANS owed to Company	$	
10. INTEREST DUE 12 months or less	$	
TOTAL		

AS AUTHORS GO

Been there, done that!

It took me 53 years to become an overnight success. Over five decades, I finally learned how to win most business matches. And while it makes me a decent trainer, I have to say that I could have thrown some early punches in my career with this information. Instead, I crawled out of the ring with cuts, bruises, and wounds in Round 2, like I did in the story. But, as with most of us stubborn fighters, I had to prove them all wrong. It took over ten years before I finally became humbled by some excellent, experienced, quietly effective trainers. In fact, I didn't have the humility, nor the ability, to identify them. Unfortunately, my business education came after I had already burned through the first four of my twenty-three companies in the seventies. When I finally did, my real career began.

My teachers were appearing for years but I never saw them. I wasn't ready. In retrospect, it was regrettable. I have scars and black eyes to prove it. There's probably not much you can tell me that I haven't experienced firsthand ten times over. I escaped business bankruptcy, but I consider my first four companies to be failures. I was thrown out of the ring early without a bit of my expected results.

I flirted with bankruptcy in the early eighties. Following the unforeseen Chapter 11s and 13s of some of my largest customers; Wickes Corporation and others, I found myself reeling and in unexpected debt overnight to the tune of $300,000 of unpaid invoices. The business I loved became my enemy. They didn't pre-warn me. I didn't foresee their situations before they were announced. I was in shock. I just couldn't tell my young family why I had sleeplessness and night sweats. I was constantly at banks, mortgaging my property, and worrying about covering large payrolls.

At that time of my career, I found myself in the air more than on the ground as I commuted weekly between offices, from Indianapolis, Indiana, to Irvine, California, to Dallas, Texas, to King of Prussia, Pennsylvania, to San Francisco, etc.

The USAir pilots knew my two sons on a first-name basis and they often let them fall asleep in the cockpit during the red-eye flights. I routinely fought through legal issues with suppliers, challenges with employees, and money problems with suppliers. My law library alone would have impressed any attorney.

Looking back after the closeout of what I thought would be my final company of 109 employees in 1995, I came to realize that I had learned a few things about business. I was weary and worn, and the welcome break of my retirement lasted four years. But, as you can see here, retirement wears many faces. The reason you would want to take what I have to say seriously is because I have probably made more mistakes in my business career than anyone you will ever know. Thank God, most were in the beginning of my career, rather than at the end.

The Genesis of Kanketa

Mike Wolf began the design of a unique eastern-based small business management system with his first business in 1965 in Milwaukee, Wisconsin. Throughout the seventies, Mike began to formulate the Kanketa principles for small businesses of thirty or less employees. In 1985, the company moved to Irvine, California, where Mike continued to experiment with Kanketa concepts.

Over fifty-three years, Mike owned twenty-three companies of every type, size, and description. His businesses were his research labs and experiments, with many hundreds of documented case studies. His employees were the trial and error people who helped along the way to prove and perfect various processes. During that time, Mike served as a consultant and speedwriter to the CEOs and senior officers of over 300 global Fortune 1,000 companies. He worked tirelessly side by side with seventy-two top executives of those companies and together, they shaped what is known today as "Kanketa, Journey in Balance."

Kanketa is the future of small business, backed by science. Today, Kanketa is making a dramatic difference in the lives of small business owners throughout the US and the world.

An Extra Free Ticket

I sincerely hope you have benefitted from this book and other Kanketa publications. If you aren't fond of stress, mystery, and guesswork about your business, we should chat. If you are no longer interested in trial and error and experimentation, and just want to make your business work once and for all, a conversation would be a good starting point. By the way, I have an extra ticket to the next match with Gitmo. I invite you to call with your toughest problems. 1-800-679-4410, ext. 1. I'll guarantee the best seat in the house.

There is one thing that you can be absolutely certain of. The Kanketa Global Team and I have nothing but your best interest in mind. Most of the money we earn after our operational expenses is invested in business education for young adults who are not college-bound and need an alternative. We prepare them for exceptional careers. AIR CAMP teaches young people more than finance and operations. At the base of its programs is **A**ccountability, **I**ntegrity, and **R**espect.

Before you close this book

Put the enclosed D-T-I forms to work in your business. At the close of every month, divide your total income by your total debts and locate your position on the Business Life Cycle to find out how safe your business is at the moment. Take a ten-cent swing at Gitmo Debt every month until you achieve $4.00 in income to every dollar in debt. When you do, the match is over.

Make D-T-I the crystal ball of your business.